LYNCHING

RACE
RHETORIC
& MEDIA

Davis W. Houck, General Editor

LYNCHING

VIOLENCE, RHETORIC, AND AMERICAN IDENTITY

ERSULA J. ORE

UNIVERSITY PRESS OF MISSISSIPPI / JACKSON

www.upress.state.ms.us

The University Press of Mississippi is a member
of the Association of University Presses.

First printing 2019

∞

Library of Congress Cataloging-in-Publication Data

Names: Ore, Ersula J., author.
Title: Lynching : violence, rhetoric, and American identity / Ersula J. Ore.
Description: Jackson : University Press of Mississippi, [2019] | Series: Race, rhetoric, and
media series | "First printing 2019." | "While victims of antebellum lynchings were typi-
cally white men, postbellum lynchings became more frequent and more intense, with the
victims more often black. After Reconstruction, lynchings exhibited and embodied links
between violent collective action, American civic identity, and the making of the nation.
Ersula J. Ore investigates lynching as a racialized practice of civic engagement. Ore scru-
tinizes the civic roots of lynching, the relationship between lynching and white constitu-
tionalism, and contemporary manifestations of lynching discourse and logic today. From
the 1880s onward, lynchings, she finds, manifested a violent form of symbolic action that
called a national public into existence, denoted citizenship, and upheld political community. Grounded in Ida B. Wells's summation of lynching as a social contract among
whites to maintain a racial order, at its core, Ore's book speaks to racialized violence
as a mode of civic engagement. Since violence enacts an argument about citizenship,
Ore construes lynching and its expressions as part and parcel of America's rhetorical
tradition and political legacy. Drawing upon newspapers, official records, and memoirs,
as well as critical race theory, Ore outlines the connections between what was said and
written, the material practices of lynching in the past, and the forms these rhetorics
and practices assume now. In doing so, she demonstrates how lynching functioned as
a strategy interwoven with the formation of America's national identity and with the
nation's need to continually restrict and redefine that identity. In addition, Ore ties black
resistance to lynching, the acclaimed exhibit Without Sanctuary, recent police brutality,
effigies of Barack Obama, and the killing of Trayvon Martin."—:Provided by publisher. |
Includes bibliographical references and index. |
Identifiers: LCCN 2018054787 (print) | LCCN 2018057399 (ebook) | ISBN 9781496821607
(epub single) | ISBN 9781496821614 (epub institutional) | ISBN 9781496821621 (pdf
single) | ISBN 9781496821638 (pdf institutional) | ISBN 9781496821591 (hardback : alk.
paper) | ISBN 9781496824080 (pbk. : alk. paper)
Subjects: LCSH: Lynching—United States—History.
Classification: LCC HV6457 (ebook) | LCC HV6457 .O74 2019 (print) | DDC 364.1/34—
dc23
LC record available at https://lccn.loc.gov/2018054787
British Library Cataloging-in-Publication Data available

To my nephew William and nieces Shelby and Kalia,
so that you may understand

A mob cannot afford to doubt: that the Jews killed Christ or that niggers want to rape their sisters or that anyone who fails to make it in the land of the free and the home of the brave deserves to be wretched. But these ideas do not come from the mob. They come from the state, which creates and manipulates the mob. The idea of black persons as property, for example, does not come from the mob. It is not a spontaneous idea. It does not come from the people, who knew better, who thought nothing of intermarriage until they were penalized for it: this idea comes from the architects of the American State.
—JAMES BALDWIN, *The Price of the Ticket*

CONTENTS

ACKNOWLEDGMENTS

This book would not have been possible without the unconditional support and guidance of many. Grandma Estelle, death has had no effect upon our connection, upon my ability to feel your presence and recognize your hand in the steps I take and the achievements I make. Thank you for your powerful prayer—for your close relationship with the Man upstairs, and for raising my mother to be a loving, wise, and, most importantly, unwearied woman. Josephine, mother, thank you for being patient with such a spirited child, for loving me enough to fight for me, for pushing past motherly resignation to encourage me to blaze a trail that was quintessentially mine. To David, my father, thank you for helping me find the words to communicate who I am and what I want to be. There are indeed *options*, Pops. I hope you're proud of the ones I've selected and the ones I've created for myself. Big Bro Joe, I thank you for setting the bar high, for being an exemplary model, and for never breaking my spirit. Thank you for showing me what individual drive, spiritual faith, and ingenuity can produce. To Kanitha, Tony, Erica, Phil, and Amanda, thank you for always loving me, for always grounding me, and for never letting me forget my worth.

This book was supported by a number of intellectual and professional relationships that continue to sustain me. Keith Gilyard modeled the kind of critical questioning and resolve that helped me see this project through and that continues to serve me today. Doc, thank you for your time, for your method, for your commitment to nurturing black intellect, and for reminding me that it's only three feet of water.

I am particularly thankful for the advice and fellowship of Rosa Eberly, the reassurance of Xioye You, and the encouragement of Cheryl Glenn during the nascent stages of this project. Phylissa Deroze, David Green, Damon Cagnolotti, Heather Brooks Adams, Michael Farris, Cara Yaa Asantewaa Christopher, Pia Deas, Una Kimokeo-Goes, Mia Briceño, Keith Miller, David Holmes, Heather Switzer, and Emir Estrada all gave formal and informal feedback that challenged and inspired me. And Elaine Richardson, Gwendolyn Pough, Tamika Carey, Daniel Brouwer, Karen Kuo, Karma Chavez, Lisa Flores, Annie Hill, and Jiyeon Kang, thank you for the years of critical engagement and dialogue, tears, and laughter; thank you all for walking alongside me as I struggled to navigate not only this project but also the indelible impression it has left upon me.

I am grateful for the institutional support provided by Arizona State University's Institute for Humanities Research (IHR) Fellowship, which supported the final stages of this project, and am especially grateful to IHR cohort members Bambi Haggins and Desirée Garcia, who kept me encouraged and inspired me to keep moving forward. I additionally want to thank the AZ Ethnic Studies Working Group and the founding members of Arizona State University's Faculty Women of Color Caucus. This project and the ones to come are a product of the advocacy and support of these organizations and the dedicated people who comprise them. Without them, I may very well not be here.

Special thanks to Randall Burkett at Emory's Stuart A. Rose Manuscript, Archives, and Rare Book Library (formerly, Emory MARBL Library) for his support, and to the various curators, outreach directors, docents, and archivists at the Charles H. Wright Museum in Detroit, Michigan; the Andy Warhol Museum in Pittsburgh, Pennsylvania; Charlotte's Levine Museum of the New South; and Cincinnati's Underground Railroad Freedom Center, who aided me during early stages of this project. Deep thanks to the University Press of Mississippi for welcoming me on board. Thank you Vijay Shah for your persistence and Craig Gill for your advocacy. Special thanks to Davis Houck for his encouragement and human kindness.

An earlier version of chapter 4 entitled, "Whiteness as Racialized Space: Barack Obama and the Rhetorical Constraints of Phenotypical Blackness," appears in Tammie Kennedy, Joyce Middleton, and Krista Ratcliffe's edited collection *Rhetorics of Whiteness: Postracial Hauntings in Popular Culture, Social Media, and Education* (Carbondale: Southern Illinois University Press, 2016), 256–70. It has been reprinted here with permission from Southern Illinois University Press.

AUTHOR'S NOTE

Lynching: Violence, Rhetoric, and American Identity is a rhetorical book, as such it gives focused attention to how language is used to perpetuate legally-sanctioned racial injustice while at the same time it uses language strategically to interrupt and disrupt the supposedly benign discourses that keep racist violence alive.[1] In this book I maintain that the violent deaths of black citizens are systemic and continuing because of implicit and often explicit approval by the state. Specific to this analysis is my rhetorical deployment of the term *murder*.[2] Although the legal definition of *murder* varies from state to state, *murder* is generally understood as the unlawful killing of a person with intent, malice, and/or premeditation. While I cannot ignore the legal definition, I do resist that this narrow frame is all the term can hold.

In this book, I sought to use the word *murder* as opposed to legal understatements such as *slaying* or *killing* because we reserve the word *murder* for the taking of human life that has value, the words *killing* or *slaying* for animals (or people) whose lives were of little use-value, and the word *slaughter* for animals when there is use-value, for us, in their destruction. In mainstream discussions of the cases analyzed in this book, the word *murder* was not generally used because the state deemed the people who died to be useless and without value. Across the book, however, I sought to use *murder* not in the legal sense, but rather to denote the killing of black people by the state. In that way, I was not speaking of individual intent only, but also naming a system that devalues and destroys black citizens through homicide. I made this rhetorical choice because there is no justice for people already presumed to be disposable, and my use of the term *murder* sought to signify the value of their lives. Murder has meaning and these murders meant something, and part of their meaning had to do with how the state justified their deaths.

While this book is grounded in a worldview resistant to an anti-black legal system that only views some killings as *murder* and others like Trayvon Martin's, Rekia Boyd's, Michael Brown's, Tamir Rice's, Philando Castile's, Korryn Gaines's, and Stephon Clark's, among others, as *justified homicides*, the word *murder* has been replaced with the words *killing*, *death*, and *slaying* in compliance with legal stipulations. As the law specifies, a sentence like "Darren Wilson *killed* Michael Brown" as opposed to "Trayvon Martin was *murdered*" is permissible because it does not slander the killer. Jurors ruled (and we can think about how such rulings have appeared in other instances of police and deputized-citizen-shootings) that neither Wilson's nor Zimmerman's pursuit and killing of Brown and Martin, respectively, was informed with the intent to kill. Because neither man set out to maliciously kill, neither man can be charged with murder or said to have committed murder. Thus, following the law, to use language—like *murder*—which asserts otherwise, potentially invites legal reprisal.

I've expelled a great deal of affective labor both in the writing of this book and this note, so I currently lack the bandwidth to elaborate on how these alterations force me to commit rhetorical violence to talk about the physical and material violence systematically enacted against blacks by the state. The lack of indictments and prevalence of acquittals that rendered these killings "lawful" reveal how justice is held by the doers of the deed—the police and deputized citizens who kill—and denied victims and their families. My thwarted effort to use *murder* rhetorically as a means of highlighting this dynamic renders me complicit with the very system of racialized power I work to critique. A chief premise of this book is that black life has value despite the ways legal code effaces black humanity. Thus, I struggle because to define Trayvon Martin's death, among others, as a *slaying* or *killing* is to dismiss the systemic nature of state-sanctioned antiblack violence, the precariousness of blackness, and the ways legally-sanctioned racial injustice sustains a racial worldview that belies claims of an America beyond race. I offer this note as testimony to the insidiousness of the law with hope that it encourages readers to reflect on the ways this book questions how we understand *intention* and *death*.

PREFACE: DEATH WISH

I had always wanted children—three, actually—but February 26, 2012, changed that; by that time it was no secret that I had resigned to not having them. While institutional harassment, the psychological toll of my work, and an ominous sense of impending doom had pretty much cemented my resignation, it was Trayvon's death, Sybrina's fight, and the way they echoed Emmett's lynching and Mamie's crusade that solidified it.

Sybrina's demand that we *see* and claim Trayvon's life as a life that mattered echoed Mamie's demand just fifty-seven years prior. There was no way I could be like Mamie or Sybrina, no way I *could not* collapse and die on site, no way I *could not* light up the Retreat; no way I could keep on fighting. I knew that I was not that kind of woman; I lacked the constitution for it.

I had children in mind when the cop car stopped me that night. It was May 20, 2014, a month after my thirty-third birthday. The day had begun like any other day. I ran through my morning routine and headed out to catch the light rail to campus. I recall thinking about this manuscript, which, unbeknown to me, had been accepted by the press the day before. I got off at Veterans Way, stopped for water and lotto tickets at the corner store on College and University, and called my father while crossing the street and heading into the office.

"Hey, Pops! Happy birthday!"

"Ers, it's not my birthday."

"What—"

"Naw. Damn, whatchu got, first-day jitters?"

"Apparently."

"Damn, girl. Either you getting old or they gettin to you, you ain't never forget my birthday." We shared a laugh. I told him about the lottery tickets, and he said to let him know when they hit. Aside from the routine inquiry about my credentials, class went off without a hitch, and I found myself making my way through campus construction and back to the light rail around 8:15 p.m.

I was on S. College Ave following the makeshift walkway that construction had laid out for pedestrians. A new building—the College University Commons—was going up, and while College Ave had been open to motorists earlier that morning, "Road Closed" signs had made the space between Sixth and Fifth Avenues a pedestrian-only thoroughfare. I followed the makeshift walkway that directed us to cross the street and had already stepped off the curb when a car entered the corridor. I waved to signal that someone was crossing and pointed to the "Road Closed" signs behind me and behind the car; it was clear that the driver hadn't seen either. He stopped when he saw me but made no attempt to turn around. I gestured again to the "Road Closed" sign behind me before asking the driver if he wanted to turn around or if I could keep crossing. He placed his elbow on the window sill, but the car remained still. I gestured again while asking, "Do you want to make a U-turn or can I cross?" but he just sat there motionless. It was late, I was hungry, and I figured that he'd seen me enough to both stop and recognize the "Road Closed" signs, so I resumed crossing the street.

It was the way he stopped me that made me think of children. Abruptly, forcefully, alarmingly. He had not been that far away, but he had thrown on the siren and raced up the street as if I were on fire. I was confused and initially thought he was racing to share news of some incident up ahead. The car stopped just at my torso, his elbow steady on the sill.

"Do you know the difference between a street and a sidewalk?"

"What?"

"Do you know the difference between a street and a sidewalk?"

Children came to mind because I knew that there was no one waiting for me at home—no child whose survival depended on me capitulating and murdering my own spirit. There was only me. Just me. And sure, family would say there had *always* been signs—that time alone in the desert had only exacerbated some maddening wish for death. But my mother knew my spirit and mind, and I knew that she would understand. I only prayed that she would forgive me for making her into the Sybrina I myself had feared becoming. I leaned back, took a breath, and spoke my piece.

"Do you always accost women in the street like this and speak to them so rudely and with such disrespect?"

While in jail I thought about those who had not made it this far, about those who ended up dead in the street, about the correlation between the state, white bodies, and bodies in blue, and about the rhetoric that would be used to discredit me. I was facing misdemeanor and felony charges that depicted me as uncivil, unruly, crazy, and dangerous. How would I convince an Arizona judge that I was in the right; that my dissent was just and legitimate—that I feared for my life?? What language would I use to make myself legible in a state that had just recently legalized racial profiling? What leverage did I have? What agency did I have? Who did I know? How would I organize? I felt like the very thing I had been writing about had come for me, had tried to silence me and put me down. What was important to me was how to fight it, how to beat it, and how to lay it bare, because the last thing I wanted to do was give America the satisfaction of knowing that it had almost killed me again.

Lynching: Violence, Rhetoric, and American Identity is both an eerie foreshadowing of what transpired May 20, 2014, and a touchstone to the maddening realities of a democratic project predicated upon the eradication of black life. On that day, Trayvon Martin was dead; Michael Brown was celebrating his eighteenth birthday; Eric Gardner, Tamir Rice, and Sandra Bland were still alive; and my father was slowly dying. The attack against me, the loss of my father, and the disproportionate number of black deaths at the hands of police and policing citizens since 2014 made completing this book an emotional and psychological quagmire. Nonetheless, I remain thankful for the ways this struggle has been a refuge and a burden. I am deeply thankful to those both near and far who have struggled and continue to struggle with me.

LYNCHING

A RHETORIC OF CIVIC BELONGING

As in torture, violence against black bodies materializes ideological beliefs.
—Christine Harold and Kevin Michael DeLuca, "Behold the Corpse"

On February 26, 2012, twenty-nine-year-old self-appointed neighborhood watchman George Zimmerman shot and killed seventeen-year-old Trayvon Martin at the Retreat, a gated community located in Sanford, Florida. According to Zimmerman, the hoodied teen armed with Skittles and an iced tea posed a grave and immediate threat to the community. In his recorded call to police, Zimmerman conjured stereotypes of the black thug when he described Trayvon as a "really suspicious guy" who was "up to no good," lamenting, "These assholes, they always get away . . . fucking coons."[1] This wasn't Zimmerman's first call to police, but instead his latest in a litany of complaints that alleged burglaries and other suspicious activity by young African American men not of the neighborhood. Like the previous forty-six calls, Zimmerman's call the night of the shooting revealed a preoccupation with policing, judgement, and keeping blacks in their place.[2] While he was not an official officer of the law, Zimmerman's role as the gun-carrying vigilante neighborhood

3

watchman imbued him with the authority of judge, jury, and executioner. Chief to Zimmerman's self-appointed role, then, was not
only discerning who belonged to the Retreat but also meting out
judgment against those who trespassed. This determination, which
was Zimmerman's alone, normally resulted in a call to local police
about suspicious activity in the neighborhood; hence, the forty-six
previous phone calls. Yet his call the night of the shooting, in which
he lamented "asshole coons" getting away with crime, suggested that
February 26, 2012, might end differently.

While the autopsy report showed that a gunshot to the chest killed
Trayvon Martin, it was the language—specifically, Zimmerman's
description of Trayvon as a black boy "up to no good"—that quickened the teen's death. Zimmerman's call to police describing Trayvon
as a "really suspicious guy" who would, like the others, "get away" (if
Zimmerman didn't intervene) invoked a sense of urgency that at
once licensed violence against Trayvon while casting Zimmerman
as the earnest and stalwart community-member protector. As a
result, Zimmerman's framing, which marked the Retreat as a certain
kind of space imagined for a certain kind of body, cast Trayvon not
only as one who did not belong but also as the enemy against which
Zimmerman must defend. From this vantage point it becomes eas-
ier to see how a jury of mostly white women—framed as potential
victims of the hoodied coon up to no good—came to determine
Zimmerman's innocence. As they concluded, Zimmerman was protecting his community from the black thug-criminal who wished to
do them harm. Profiling Trayvon to his death, then, was neither racist nor murderous, but rather an act of community, one that unfor-
tunately resulted in the death of a black boy.

On July 13, 2013 Zimmerman was found innocent on all counts.
Many who read the verdict as a miscarriage of justice were disturbed
by the way Trayvon's killing and Zimmerman's acquittal mirrored
the 1955 lynching of Emmett Louis Till and the acquittal of his murderers, Roy Bryant and J. W. Milam. During an August 2013 interview
for her upcoming movie, *The Butler*, Oprah drew what she described

as a "parallel" between the two, saying Trayvon Martin, Emmett Till "Let me just tell you: in my mind, same thing."[3] Oprah was neither the first nor the last to draw this conclusion.[4] Political pundits, congressmen, and celebrities, including legendary actor and longtime social activist Harry Belafonte, agreed that "the corollary between the two tragedies" was undeniable.[5] Critics, however, denounced the claim as hyperbolic, asserting that the incidents were drastically different. According to Sean Hannity, the killing of Trayvon Martin and the murder of Emmett Till were different because, unlike Emmett's murder, Trayvon's "wasn't about race," "even Trayvon Martin's family and attorney said it wasn't about race!"[6] To make such a "unbelievably wrong" and "offensive" comparison, argued Hannity, was to engage in what one critic defined as "idiocy and racial poison."[7] Glenn Beck declared similarly, explaining that Emmett was tortured and killed because he was meant to exemplify the consequences of flirting with a white woman, whereas Trayvon was killed because he was a suspicious-looking character who was out late at night and up to no good.[8] The two incidents, critics argued, were distinct in form and motive: Emmett's murder was a lynching because it was a racially motivated act of torture and killing, while Trayvon's death, which involved neither torture nor racist intent, was simply an act of self-defense. Such colorblind critiques asserted three things: that form superseded motive in determination of guilt, that claims of self-defense were fundamentally devoid of racist intent, and that a killing was a lynching only if the killing involved racially motivated torture like that sustained by Emmett. Such narrow definitions for what constitutes a lynching permitted conservatives to deny the continuity between Trayvon and Emmett's slayings and to conclude that those who read Trayvon and Emmett as "the same thing" were more interested in stoking the fires of racial divide than in encouraging racial unity.[9]

I recall the controversy over the Emmett–Trayvon comparison for the way it highlights continued debate over the definition of lynching and the ways such debate reflects an ongoing tradition to rhetorically save face through denial of lynching's adaptive and transformative nature. The rhetoric of shame and blame used to combat lynching contributed to its decline during the late 1930s and the advent of a discourse characterized by a narrower definition of lynching, which proponents used to deny the continued practice of lynching during the 1940s onward. What Ashraf Rushdy termed the "end-of-lynching discourse" was forwarded by organizations like the Association of Southern Women for the Prevention of Lynching (ASWPL), which called for a narrower definition of lynching under the guise that the historical context in which lynchings had occurred had ended. Opponents of this discourse, like the National Association for the Advancement of Colored People (NAACP), which called for a more "capacious and flexible definition"[10] of lynching, contended that "lynchings were part of a larger pattern of vigilante and extralegal violence in American history, and that changes after the 1930s marked a transformation, not a termination, in that history."[11] Forwarding a "narrower definition of what constituted a lynching," then, permitted proponents of the end-of-lynching discourse "to deny that a given event—which might previously have been identified as a lynching— was one."[12] Such masking, explains Rushdy, sought to rescue white America from being further stigmatized by anti-lynching rhetoric that collapsed lynching and national identity.[13]

Today, the campaign to save face and rescue whiteness through rhetorical frames that deny lynching continues. Those refuting that Trayvon and Emmett were the same thing invoked this discursive history and strategy to assert that if the racially motivated kidnapping, torture, murder, and impromptu "hanging" of an innocent black boy was a "lynching," then Trayvon's death, which was neither racially motivated nor involved the impromptu hanging of an innocent boy, was not the same thing. Critics' characterization of Trayvon and Emmett also contributed to their contention that the killing of the two boys was distinctly different. Characterizations of the two turned on a distorted sense of agency—specifically, Emmett's lack of agency as a *victim* of racism and Trayvon's perceived agency as a

racial *aggressor*. These characterizations constructed frames of guilt
and innocence that permitted critics to reject the ways systemic
racism informed the boys' deaths and readings of their killings as
"the same thing." The narrative forwarded by conservatives depicted
Emmett as a relatively innocent but boastful youth, and Trayvon as
a troublemaker and thug who, as Beck parroted, told Zimmerman
that "he was going to die tonight."[14] Following this logic, the boys'
deaths are not united by race or the spectacular form each killing
took, because the incidents are additionally distinguished by the
character of the decedents. Essentially, Emmett was innocent and
meant no harm, whereas Trayvon got what he deserved, because, as
Beck explained, Trayvon was up to no good.

To assert that the Trayvon-is-Emmett comparison lacks validity
on account of form, motive, and character is to reject the changing same that is American racism. To reject the parallels uniting
Trayvon and Emmett in life and death is to likewise deny how critical black memory like that exhibited by Oprah, Belafonte, and others has functioned and continues to function as a political resource
that combats racial oppression by making "visible what has been
obscured, what has been excluded and what has been forgotten."[15]
Reading the "shooting death" of Trayvon Martin and the lynching of
Emmett Till as "the same thing," then, is not hyperbolic. On the contrary, it is quite astute. Such a reading reflects a critical democratic
literacy specific to the condition of being black in America, how
blacks use memory to negotiate the present, and a way of deliberat-
ing with others that reflects an attunement to "ethical evaluations of
the past" and "living engagement with the past."[16]

Trayvon's death was a modern-day lynching. I say this not to be
provocative but because it is true. From the language used to ratio-
nalize Zimmerman's actions to the logic and outcome of the trial,
the story of Trayvon Martin and George Zimmerman exhibits how
the logic, discourse, and practice of American lynching have been
adapted in the twenty-first century in ways that sustain a democratic
project predicated upon the circumscription and eradication of

black life. A major feature of lynching discourse, reminds Jesse Carr, involves the strategic use of language and symbols that "constitute broad norms against which figures of perversion can be produced," figures like the black beast rapist, black brute, black thug, and threating Negro, which become the "ultimate Others who are appropriate targets of lynch law."[17] Like lynchings of the past, Trayvon's exhibited language that criminalized blackness. Trayvon wasn't the black boy walking home in the rain, but rather the hoodied asshole, the black burglar, and dark threat that did not belong. Zimmerman's choice to describe Trayvon as the "suspicious coon up to no good" framed the unarmed black teen as a perversion of the norms constituting the Retreat and, consequently, an appropriate target for lynching.

Another major feature of lynching was the assumed innocence of the lyncher and the aid of law enforcement in the lynching, either as active members of the mob or through acquiescence to it. Accounts of lynching frequently implicate law enforcement and other branches of the justice system as agents of the mob. Mainstream news reports often exposed how officers halfheartedly defended victims when the mob came for them and, in other instances, actively assisted in the spectacle by providing keys to holding cells.[18] From 1880 to 1930, lynchers in Georgia lynched 80 percent of victims seized from law officers, while lynchers in Virginia lynched 94 percent of the victims seized from authorities.[19] Despite the public nature of spectacle lynchings, lynchers were rarely ever indicted or tried, and in the event that they were, were rarely ever convicted for their crimes. As Arthur Raper reports,

> In six of the twenty-one lynchings of 1930 . . . grand jury indictments were returned against a total of forty-nine persons. In the other fifteen instances, the coroners reported that the lynched persons came to their deaths "at the hands of persons unknown" to them. The grand juries in turn failed to fix responsibility. Of the forty-nine persons indicted only four have been convicted. At Herman, two received sentences of two years each, being convicted of arson and rioting rather than of murder.[20]

Raper's record offers just one of the many ways that law enforcement and other branches of the justice system endorsed lynching. Like lynchers of the past, Zimmerman was never arrested, held, or investigated following Trayvon's death but instead walked freely for forty-four days before Florida officials yielded to national pressure to indict him.[21] Failure to enact standard investigative procedures in the death of Trayvon Martin and the lack of procedure that led officers to display Trayvon's uncovered body for hours, were chief features of this twenty-first-century spectacle lynching.

Third, like lynchings of the past, Trayvon's rendered the hunting, trapping, and killing of blacks in the twenty-first century not simply reasonable, but legally *just*. Lynchings and pro-lynching discourse commonly used tropes of the hunt to normalize lynching as a practice of subsistence and survival.[22] Zimmerman called upon this discursive history when he dismissed dispatch's directions to stay in his car and instead got out on foot to hunt Trayvon to his death. As Zimmerman demonstrated, he was more interested in stalking, trapping, and subduing Trayvon than in heeding the law. Similar still to lynchings of the past was how the predominantly white and female jury disregarded these facts and selected instead to read Zimmerman's pursuit of Trayvon as an act of self-defense, as opposed to one of recklessness and/or malicious intent. The final verdict, which found Zimmerman innocent, affirmed that citizens driven by racial paranoia and antiblack sentiment had a greater right to life than those whom they imagined to be dangerous. In this way, the jury's verdict, like verdicts of the past, enacted the same depraved indifference to black life that motivated Zimmerman to pursue Trayvon to his death in the first place. Trayvon Martin died not only once, then, but twice: once by Zimmerman's hand and again at the hands of the jury.

Lastly, like lynchings of the past, Trayvon's lynching turned on a logic of black criminality and white vulnerability that allowed Zimmerman to perform whiteness through his removal of the hoodied coon that did not belong. This last point is key. Although not white, Zimmerman's decision to pursue Trayvon to his death combined a historically white way of seeing and reading blacks as always already criminal with the historically white right to kill blacks with impunity. As bell hooks and George Yancy remind, the right to look—let alone *look, judge,* and *act*—has, since the instantiation of the nation, been the sole privilege of Americans with white racial standing.[23] Enacting this historical right, then, was a performance of whiteness that linked Zimmerman to a larger tradition of lynching, white supremacy, black death, and national identity.

Although Zimmerman was not white, his language and symbolic labor as judge, jury, and executioner invoked a tradition of antiblack violence and racial solidarity that coded him as white. This logic was further reinforced in the selection of an all-woman, predominantly white jury and a case for the defense that equated blackness to threat, white femininity to innocence, and white masculinity to chivalry through tactics that included showing the jury images of white women meant to represent female victims from the Retreat. Such tactics sought to encourage the predominantly white and female jury to read Zimmerman as the gallant savior of white women while simultaneously inviting them to rhetorically identify with the myth of feminine virtue and white vulnerability. Encouraging jurors to imagine themselves as the very white victims portrayed by the defense was not only an appeal to sanction the racially motivated killing of a seventeen-year-old black boy but also an appeal to community, one in which jurors imagined Zimmerman as the ultimate model citizen. There is only one tradition that describes the conscious choice to profile a black boy to death as chivalrous, only one tradition that posits the conscious eradication of black life as an unfortunate, but nonetheless ugly, consequence of supposed black delinquency, and only one tradition that uses racial terror as a means of policing the boundaries between America's white "us" and its black "them": that tradition— what Ida B. Wells referred to as America's "national crime"—is lynching.[24] It was Zimmerman's enactment of this tradition that permitted the defense to construct the Retreat as the rhetorical stand-in for the nation and Zimmerman as the valiant protector of vulnerable white Americans. Trayvon Martin's "shooting death" is a lynching, then, because it invoked not only the same rhetoric and rationale as lynchings but also the same outcome: the legally sanctioned eradication of black life.

Lynching: Violence, Rhetoric, and American Identity draws connections between the rhetorics and material practices of lynching in the past and the forms these rhetorics and practices assume in the present to outline how the debasement and eradication of black life prevail today as vehicles of democratic citizenship. Lynching has been a constitutive performance of American civic identity since the eighteenth century, when its debut as a punitive response to British Tories during the American Revolution set the stage for its later development as a violent rhetoric of American citizenship.[25] During the eighteenth century, lynching was deployed by Virginia magistrate Charles Lynch as a means of safeguarding the nation against British allies. America's war for independence created exigencies for which Lynch, a commissioned colonel, had to respond—the most pressing of which were the stealing and selling of local horses to British forces, and plots of insurgency against prominent Virginia patriots. Because local courts were only examining courts, and the closest court to assess felonies was over two hundred miles away, Lynch was forced to adapt. With the aid of his posse, Lynch established a local court system in which he as presiding justice, and his posse as fellow magistrates of the peace, meted out justice. Although Lynch's court was not an official regulatory entity, it nonetheless retained features common in demonstrations of state power. Judgment of the accused appealed to communal notions of morality and justice, confessions were solicited from the accused, and the guilty were punished before the eyes of the public. Lynch's court was, for all intents and purposes, a court whose judgment aimed to protect America from threat by expelling the enemy within. In doing so, lynch law not only secured the borders of America but defined who was, and who was not, a member of the burgeoning new nation.

The rhetorical power of colonial lynchings turned on their capacity to unify early Americans through violent public action, shared
sentiment, and an imagining of "the people" as a politically sovereign
body, as opposed to British "subjects." Tories represented diseased
organisms within a nascent body politic. Subduing this "enemy
within" through both physical and symbolic forms of expulsion,
then, helped to alleviate anxiety over an imposing threat while at
the same time fostering a sense of shared identity among colonials.
Lynching served, then, as a political and symbolic curative: expelling the enemy within helped to alleviate the people's anxiety over
the war while at the same time strengthen the fictive bonds of kin-
ship—those imagined notions of an "us"—underwriting American
identity.[26] Under these conditions, lynch law became an expression
of national loyalty that made the lyncher, justices, and supporters of
Lynch's court synonymous with the American loyalist and facilitated
a sense of collective identity among "the people." "The Dogwood
Tree" poem[27] and the familiar axiom "Hurrah for Colonel Lynch,
Captain Bob and Callaway! They never turned a Tory loose, until he
cried out 'Liberty'" was an early cultural expression that cast lynching and its practitioners as pursuant of democracy.[28] As a putative
mechanism of justice sanctioned by the people, lynch law became
indelibly linked to expressions of American civic identity; individuals who agreed to be governed by a shared set of principles were in
turn endowed with the power to judge and mete out punishment
against those they deemed a threat to their way of life.

Lynching during the American Revolution expressed ideals of
popular sovereignty that framed the practice as "the people's" right
to enforce a democratic ideal in lieu of those who posed a threat to
the pursuit of American independence.[29] As historian Frank Shay
explains, "in those early days an informer [British loyalist] was
invariable in the service of the crown and therefore anathema to all
patriots who, when he was unmasked, undertook to flog him and to
hold him up to popular exposure and contempt."[30] Tories became
emblems of national contempt and suffered a combination of pub-

lic flogging, tarring, feathering, imprisonment, fines, expulsion, and hanging.[31] Communal spirit characterized the flogging and "lynching" of political enemies and legitimated the assumed autonomy of colonials to mete out justice. Tories were the "enemy within"—the political other against which Americans defined, and through collective support for judgment of Tories and violence against them, reinforced their own political identities as well as the boundaries of the polity. In this way, lynching was the enactment of an argument—one that articulated American identity as anti-British and wholly opposed to tyranny. Under these conditions lynching became a practice of political affiliation that differentiated America's "us" from Britain's "them," a vehicle through which Americans communicated a sense of belonging and national identity.

Worth noting is how Lynch's Court was, at one point, contested because accused Tories were never tried following proper due process of law. To begin, county records show an alarmingly high number of guilty pleas for counts of treason. Such frequency suggests that confessions were compelled under duress rather than willingly given.[32] Additionally, correspondence between Colonel Lynch and Gov. Thomas Jefferson reveal the governor's reservations about Lynch's methods. Acknowledging the extenuating circumstances that necessitated an "unofficial" felonies court, Jefferson nonetheless pressed Lynch on the need to remain lawful and to ensure that defendants "be regularly tried [as in a "proper" court of law] afterwards."[33] The governor's overture to observe "the law" is noteworthy. Jefferson was a stickler for order and decorum, yet his directions to Lynch seemed to point more toward the need to observe purviews of state power so as to ensure that Lynch's action—that is, lynching—was legally defensible, than toward a view of lynching as unethical or activity unauthorized by the state.

Lynch and his outfit were never reprimanded for their actions. When brought before the General Assembly on counts of illegal activity, he and his justices were exonerated, and Lynch was later appointed to the court of uncommon pleas, colonial America's equivalent to the court of appeals.[34] During their trial the assembly ruled that although the group's actions may not have been "strictly warranted by law," lynching was nevertheless justifiable and appropriate, given the threat Tories and the rising insurgency posed to the surrounding community. The trial resulted in legislation that deputized citizens to pursue and suppress perceived insurgents under the guise of national security,[35] and in defining lynching as legal, venerable action reflective of one's deep commitment to the nation and investment in protecting its ideas. The Act to Indemnify Certain Persons in Suppressing a Conspiracy against the State commended Lynch's court:

> Charles Lynch and other *faithful citizens*, aided by detachments of volunteers from different parts of the state, did, by timely and effectual measures, suppress such conspiracy. . . . Be It Therefore Enacted, That the said William Preston, Robert Adams, junior, James Callaway, and Charles Lynch, and all other persons whatsoever, concerned in suppressing said conspiracy, or in advising, issuing or executing any orders, or measures taken for that purpose, stand indemnified and exonerated of and from all pains, penalties, prosecutions, actions, suites, and damages on account thereof.[36]

What Lynch's court did, concluded the assembly, was protect the welfare of the state and, by extension, the nation. Such patriotism—such national service—was to be lauded, not questioned, and certainly not penalized. The precedent set by Virginia's legislature left an indelible impression on the practice of American civics; Lynch's exoneration and later promotion legitimated lynching as an integral part of American civic life.

The assembly's ruling produced three notable outcomes. First, it placed lynching within the purview of the law by framing it as a wartime measure aimed at stamping out insurgents and conspirators. This meant that lynching was not unsanctioned violence performed beyond the authority of the law, and therefore *extralegal activity*.

Rather the legislature's decision to pardon Lynch's court situated *lynch law* within the province of America's budding judicial system. Second, exonerating Lynch and his assistants cast lynching as legally protected action. As the assembly ruled, lynching was a *just* and therefore legitimate way of preserving American life. This precedent is particularly noteworthy given the rarity with which lynchers of the nineteenth century were indicted and convicted, and the logic used to legitimate their acts as venerable performances of citizenship. Whether it was an act of popular justice or not, the court ruled that lynching was praiseworthy, legally sanctioned action that reflected the "best" and "leading" qualities of civic identity. By framing lynching as both "patriotic service" and "service" performed on behalf of and for the "good" of "the people," the legislature birthed a legitimating discourse that would later be appropriated by pro-lynching communities of the late nineteenth, twentieth, and twenty-first centuries.

Third, the Assembly's ruling rendered lynching exemplary citizenly etiquette and situated it as necessary and acceptable action taken by those guided by a resounding sense of civic responsibility and national identity. This logic reasoned that those who lynched did so out of service to the nation and for the good of the American people. Such logic cast Lynch and his posse as "leading citizens" of America's burgeoning national community and rendered the patriot synonymous with the lyncher, and the lyncher synonymous with the *ultimate faithful citizen*. Lynch's later appointment to the court of uncommon pleas solidified the synonymous relationship between the lyncher and the "leading" or exemplary citizen, while his acquittal, praise, and subsequent promotion to the highest court within the colonial juridical system rendered lynching a species of American jurisprudence. Lynching, then, while a performance of exceptional citizenship, does not constitute a state of exception in that it embodies an instance in which the law is momentarily suspended, but rather represents an instance in which the logic and spirit of American democracy are enacted. As such, lynching shares a relationship of interiority with American law, the formation of the nation, and the constitution of "the people."

Prior to Reconstruction, an anxious and fretful slave society used lynching as a way of enforcing adherence to a racialized democratic ideal. Accounts of lynchings during slavery are sparse but have been noted during instances in which slaves transgressed boundaries between property and personhood. Insurrectionist acts such as murdering masters, raping mistresses, and planning rebellions warranted lynching because they threatened the generational perpetuation of white supremacy while at the same time redefining the subhuman slave as the fully human master.[37] Lynchings that occurred in this context were violent performances of reclamation that reaffirmed white supremacy through the disavowal of black humanity. Lynchings after Reconstruction continued this trend in the way they differentiated America's white "us" from its black "them." Democratic citizenship during the antebellum period conceived "the people" as a "whites only" collective, and citizenship as the right to enforce white dominance. These changes, which included transforming the black slave into the black citizen, "triggered more intense cultural differentiation of blackness and whiteness as whites strove to fortify the color line and consolidate white identity in order to protect white supremacy."[38] Harsh codes like the black codes of 1865–1866, which restricted a variety of civil liberties for blacks following emancipation, were the first line of defense against black citizenship. Lynching was the second.

From the postbellum period to our contemporary time, lynching as both a material practice and a rhetorical performance has exhibited an ideological belief regarding black inferiority, white superiority, and the need to keep blacks in their racially prescribed place. This need, I argue, is a condition of the color-line logic underwriting legislation that codified antiblack sentiment and antiblack violence as etiquettes of American identity. Color-line logic adopts W. E. B. Du Bois's oft-quoted observation about race in America for the purpose of highlighting how lynching and other forms of antiblack violence reflect the racial-spatial order of the *racial contract.* What political philosopher Charles Mills defines as the racial contract denotes the white racist logic of classic contractarianism, which espouses a race-neutral theory of politics via a hidden transcript of white supremacy. Mills's theory of the racial contract unveils this transcript to illustrate how the social contract—that tacit agreement among men to leave the state of nature and enter into the reason-governed space of civic life—is not in actuality "a contract between everybody ('we the people'), but between just the people who count, the people who really are ('we the white people')."[39] The racial contract, then, is a "contract between those categorized as white *over* the nonwhites, who are thus the objects rather than subjects of the agreement" to maintain a "racial polity, a racial state, and a racial judicial system."[40] To be a subject of the racial contract is to be vulnerable to its subsidiary agreements such as the *expropriation contract,* which permitted white settlers to claim sovereign power over native lands, the *slavery contract,* which "gave Europeans the right to enslave Native Americans and Africans at a time when slavery was dead or dying in Europe," and the *colonial contract,* which "legitimated European rule over the nations in Asia, Africa, and the Pacific."[41]

Spatializing DuBois's theory, Mills asserts that "[p]art of the purpose of the color bar; the color line/ apartheid/jim crow is to maintain" the space of "the people"—that is, civic space—as space for "whites only," so as to keep them—blacks (those "anticitizens" and enemies of the social contract[42])—"in their place."[43] This study of lynching, violence, rhetoric, and American identity, then, acknowledges the historical truth of the racial contract as an agreement among whites—tacit or otherwise—to "maintain and reproduce [a] racial order"[44] through laws and customs that preserve a racial hierarchy that privileges whiteness and that rhetorically and ontologically excludes nonwhites "from the promise of 'the liberal project of modernity.'"[45] Consequently, *Lynching: Violence, Rhetoric, and American Identity* reads lynching as a violent rhetorical performance that enacts the color-line logic of the racial contract.

Here I echo Ida B. Wells's formulation of lynching as an agreement among whites to maintain a white racial order, as it lays the
foundation for my interpretation of lynching as a performance of
American identity. The investigative journalist, businesswoman, and
spearhead of the anti-lynching movement exposed the underpin-
nings of lynching to reveal that lynching had nothing to do with
regulating black criminality or safeguarding the honor of white
women from lascivious black beasts. The singular focus of lynching, explained Wells, was to nullify the constitutional rights of black
citizens—more specifically, of black men—through raced and gendered codes that framed white women as worthy of protection from
rape and black women as "wonton, licentious," and "promiscuous"
women who could not be raped on account that they were already
"'bad' women."[46] Asserting that lynching enacted white rejection to
the civic prosperity of blacks exposed what blacks had long understood, namely, that antiblack violence was not aberrant to America's
ways but a constitutive practice of them and its people. Following
this framework, when Wells asserted that lynching was America's
"national crime," she was in part arguing that lynching was proof
that democracy wasn't about maintaining equality among "the people," but instead about maintaining equality among the only people
who counted—that is, white people.

Government indifference to the plight of black citizens and failure to pass anti-lynching legislation further corroborated Wells's
contention that lynching was a manifestation of the racial contract. America was "active and outspoken in its endeavors to right
the wrongs" committed against humans abroad, she noted, yet
conveniently failed to enact such compassion when similar atrocities impacted citizens of color.[47] *Lynching: Violence, Rhetoric, and
American Identity* builds on Wells's insights to examine the interpretive and symbolic work of lynching from the 1880s onward, and the
ways the lynched black body has indexed and continues to index the
ongoing struggle over the meanings and boundaries of American
identity in the United States. What I refer to here as color-line logic,

then, reflects not only the way lynching, and contemporary manifestations of lynching such as antiblack police brutality, racializes civic space as space for whites only, but moreover how such performances work to maintain a racial polity and a racial state in the midst of our supposedly postracial condition.

Citizenship and Belonging

Citizenship is commonly thought of as the active participation of social actors in civic life. Exercising the right to vote, the right to freedom of speech, and the right to assembly are a customary performance of citizenship that mark individuals as members of the polity. Such performances are ideologically bound ways of enacting our sense of "place" and belonging within an imagined community[48] and, at the same time, performances of how we as social actors imagine our political world. Although congressional Reconstruction legally marked blacks as citizens endowed with the same rights and protections as their white counterparts, the successful performance of whiteness, which coincided with the continuance of a white civic order, remained grounded in the racial expectation of black acquiescence to white dominance.[49] Such performative expectations reproduced and sustained whiteness as the epitome of Americanness by wielding lynching as a constitutive performance of American identity.

Scholars generally discuss lynching as a mark of civic exclusion, noting in particular how it thrived following Reconstruction because emancipated slaves remained unprotected by citizenship laws at the end of the nineteenth century.[50] Lynching was a form of social control that maintained the racial status quo through its denial of due process of law. By denying black victims the right to due process, lynchers were in fact arguing that the protections and privileges of American citizenship were the exclusive rights of the white men and women who lynched them. These "drama[s] of intrusion by and protection from external enemies,"[51] then, became rhetorically constitutive occasions in which American civic identity was affirmed through antiblack violence, violence informed by an ideological belief that blacks "had no rights which the white man was bound to respect."[52] Cynthia Skove Nevels's examination of lynching culture in Brazos County, Texas, at the beginning of the twentieth century examines how eastern and southern European immigrants socially and politically transcended their marginalization by participating in collective acts of antiblack oppression and violence. "Lynching to belong," as she called it, permitted Brazos County immigrants to secure their social and political welfare by participating in the further marginalization of black citizens.[53] Such collective action delineated citizenship in the way it united immigrants and white Texans along a shared spectrum of intelligibility that marked immigrants as citizens of Brazos County's white community, blacks as those who did not belong, and lynching as a constitutive performance of white identity and civic belonging.

Scholars have also given attention to how feminine constructions of the nation inform lynching's civic character. As Dora Apel explains, racism "produced a conflation of political and sexual fears that regarded the political enfranchisement of black men as a catalyst to the 'rape' of white women."[54] Such logic asserted that citizenship emboldened black depravity, which in turn contributed to white vulnerability. Sandy Alexandre, echoing insights from scholars such as Elizabeth Hale White and Jacqueline Goldsby, likewise noted how discourse of the black beast rapist and the fair white maiden metonymically constructed the white female body as the physical embodiment of the nation. Tropes determining the bodies and sexuality of white women "to be vulnerable to (black) attack," came to "presage the very vulnerability of the nation itself," explains Alexandre.[55] Metonymically constructing white women as America's national body, then, figured white men as the ultimate citizen-savior while at the same time casting lynching as a performance of virtuous citizenship. The fact that similar figurations permeate the discourse and logic used to acquit George Zimmerman is yet another reverberation of the past that makes it difficult to interpret Trayvon's lynching as a "shooting death." The fact that similar figurations continue to permeate the discourse and logic used to acquit police officers and private citizens of racially motivated violence illustrates a continued indifference to black humanity in the twenty-first century.

Lynching was a call to communion, a performance of political affiliation akin to citizenship in the way it distinguished those who belonged from those who did not. Literally and symbolically rescinding the civic rights of African Americans so as to return them to their "rightful place" outside the polity nurtured a democracy in which overtly legal protections around racial oppression were the norm. This is to say, then, that lynching evidenced that the particular suit of rights and privileges associated with American identity were the exclusive rights and privileges of "whites only." As an open and public display of power, lynchings united audience members along a shared experience of spectatorship that made them complicit in the act as they looked on, chanted, and cheered alongside the cries of their victims. The sheer volume of the crowd, the push and pull of closely packed bodies along a jailhouse yard, town square, or courthouse lawn further enhanced the constitutive power of lynching by not only creating a sense of "belonging and commonality that sustained the violence"[56] but also producing an image of solidarity and belonging that simultaneously functioned as an epideictic text.

Epideictic rhetoric denotes discourse that persuades through modes of display, exhibition, and demonstration. Epideictic rhetoric is known as a rhetoric of display and might best be described as a "species of pedagogy"[57] that instructs those addressed in the ways of the community through modes of exhibition and demonstration. Both the lynching spectacle and the lynched black body functioned epideictically as displays of American identity. While the lynching spectacle modeled attitudes and practices deemed fundamentally "American,"[58] the lynched black body instructed citizens across the color line in modes of engagement that rendered "white" synonymous with "American" while simultaneously maintaining and reproducing white supremacy as the democratic norm. Lynching photographs, lynching postcards, and corporeal keepsakes such as burned hair and fingers from lynching victims allowed those unable to attend the spectacle the opportunity to be equally inculcated as a member of a larger imagined community. Such models helped individuals locate themselves within America's prophetic grand narrative and, in so doing, mark themselves as those who *belonged*. My exploration of lynching as a violent rhetoric of American identity, then, attends to the ways the discourse and practice of lynching imparted vital lessons about civics to citizens along the color line, and the ways those lessons continue to reverberate in the present.

Why Lynching? Why Now?

Lynching is largely thought to be a part of America's long-ago past as opposed to its immediate present. This is in part due to the culture of silence and shame that contributed to the decline of American lynching during the 1930s and in part to the advent of "end-of-lynching discourse in the 1940s.[59] Prior to the 1930s, anti-lynching advocates defined lynching through focused attention to questions around guilt, complicity, and social responsibility. While advocates agreed that lynching must be stopped, they had difficulty agreeing on what constituted a lynching. As Rushdy explains, early debates over the definition of lynching exhibited a distinction between *form* and *motive*—advocates focused on form defined lynching as a practice comprising "a narrow ambit [sic] of guilty actors (the Samaritan model)," while advocates focused on motive proposed "an expanded range of responsibility" that rendered spectators equally complicit with lynchers in the act.[60] Focused attention on form over motive reflected greater investment in recuperating a damaged national ethos than safeguarding the lives of black citizens.

> Because lynching had for so long been a barometer of race relations,
> the decline of lynching had come to be desired *primarily* for what

that decline would indicate about the state of the nation. A lynch-free year . . . meant a year that America had become better and less racist . . . that we lived in a new era, or at least not in a past or bygone one.[61]

It is partly because of this rhetorical campaign to save face that the killings of Amadou Diallo (1999), Patrick Dorismond (2000), Trayvon Martin (2012), Eric Garner (2014), Michael Brown (2014), Tamir Rice (2014), Samuel DuBose (2015), Walter Scott (2015), Keith Scott (2016), Philando Castile (2017), and Stephon Clark (2018), among others, are defined as instances of "self-defense," "legal shooting," or "benign" policing as opposed to lynchings.

In its 2016 report, the United Nations' Working Group of Experts on People of African Descent declared antiblack police brutality to be part of America's tradition of lynching. Defining lynching as "a form of racial terrorism that has contributed to a legacy of racial inequality that the US must address," the panel concluded that "contemporary killings and the trauma it creates are reminiscent of the racial terror lynchings of the past. Impunity for state violence has resulted in the current human rights crisis and must be addressed as a matter of urgency."[62] The panel's conclusions reinforced findings from a similar report issued by Montgomery, Alabama's Equal Justice Initiative (EJI), a research and advocacy group that challenges racial injustice through its work to eradicate mass incarceration and excessive punishment, and its activism on behalf of marginalized and impoverished communities.[63] Chief to its mission is educating policy makers on the ways America's history of lynching continues to impact African Americans. In "Lynching in America: Confronting the Legacy of Racial Terror," the EJI detailed the ways lynching "shaped the contemporary geographic, political, social, and economic conditions of African Americans" and how "[m]ass incarceration, racially biased capital punishment, excessive sentencing, disproportionate sentencing of racial minorities," and antiblack policing reveal how contemporary race relations have been "shaped by the terror era."[64]

Like those of the past, contemporary proponents of end-of-lynching discourse focus on form as opposed to motive as a means of disrupting the continuity between America's "terror era" and the forms such terrorism takes today. The May 2017 killing of Richard Collins III at the University of Maryland exhibits this interpretative practice. Collins was standing at a campus bus stop with friends when Sean Urbanski, a University of Maryland student and white supremacist, stabbed him. Collins, a soon-to-be graduate of Bowie State University, was to start his commission as a second lieutenant in the U.S. Army later that May. When *The Nation*'s Dave Zirin referred to Collins's death as a lynching, he was summarily challenged. According to critics, Collins's death wasn't a lynching because Urbanski didn't use a rope to kill him; he used a knife.[65] Historical ignorance aside (lynchings consisted of shootings, stabbings, and burnings as well as hangings), the preoccupation with form evidenced in the "knife over rope" rationale, dismisses the motive that links Collins's killing to the historical and systemic practice of lynching and that practice to a tradition of American identity.

The August 2017 "wounding" of a biracial eight-year-old in Claremont, New Hampshire, offers another iteration of this discourse. Quincy and his eleven-year old sister, Ayanna, were playing with four white boys when the boys decided to enact a lynching. Parents of a white teen accused of lynching Quincy said their son never encouraged the fourth-grader to get on the table and put his head in the noose, and that once it was around his head, never pushed the boy and let him hang. They also denied that their son, along with others, used racial slurs and threw rocks and sticks at Quincy days prior to the incident.[66] According to thirty-three-year-old Rhianna Larkin and thirty-two-year-old Eric Sullivan, their eleven-year-old-son was innocent because they had not raised him to hold racist views or to treat black members of their family differently. Larkin cited her father's half-sisters and her boyfriend's sister-in-law as proof that her son wasn't racist.[67] As she explained, it was a "complete backyard accident," there was no racial animus involved.[68] Here, preoccupation with form—"this is not a lynching, but rather just boys playing"—manifests as a semantic move to save face.

Rhianna Larkin's "we can't be racist because we have black family" rationale—which is offered as proof of her son's good moral character—dismisses the perception that race had any bearing on his actions. As Rhianna explained, this couldn't be a lynching because her son doesn't see race.[69]

Like those of the past, contemporary opponents of end-of-lynching discourse contended that lynching merely changed as opposed to ended. In an opinion piece on the hanging of eight-year-old Quincy, interracial parents Sindiso Minsi Weeks and Dan Weeks of New Hampshire highlighted how mainstream news outlets avoided calling the event "by its name" despite reports of taunting by the boys who allegedly hanged Quincy, despite the ways these alleged tormentors enacted white solidarity and belonging in their shared act of racially motivated violence against Quincy, and despite the ways police indifference to the pursuit of justice for Quincy mimicked the past.[70] According to the Weekses, what happened in Claremont was not a wounding or a hanging; it was an "attempted lynching."[71]

Reporter Dave Zirin, in "Why I Called the Murder of Richard Collins III a Lynching," asserted that calling Collins's death by name was

important both definitionally and politically. . . . If we don't see Richard Collins III in the centuries-old continuum of lynchings, we are helping whitewash what took place. We are categorizing what happened as an aberration in the "post-racial" 21st-century United States. . . . To say otherwise obscures the fact that this living tradition of violent white supremacy is currently being nurtured from the campus to cable news to the White House."[72]

While the trial against Sean Urbanski in the killing of Richard Collins III is scheduled to begin later this year, the verdicts of so many other trials featuring the killing of innocent black men have already been delivered. The general consensus regarding the precepts of American democracy is that they were deficient in practice

but perfect in notion—impacted most ardently by human imper-
fection as opposed to human conceptualization. The experienced
reality of democracy, however, is not that it is imperfect, but that its
imperfections strategically target members of the polity not originally conceived as members of the polity. My purpose in *Lynching:
Violence, Rhetoric, and American Identity*, then, is to center lynching
as a material and rhetorical performance that illustrates the mutually constitutive relationship between democracy and antiblack
violence. In doing so I aim to demonstrate the ways lynching and
its rhetorics have been and remain interwoven both with the formation of America's national identity and with the nation's need to
continually renew that identity.

Like lynchings in the past, lynchings at the turn of the twenty-
first century continue to characterize American identity and citizenship belonging as the ability to kill blacks with impunity.[73]
While officers and civilians responsible for the "shooting deaths" of
Amadou Diallo (1999), Patrick Dorismond (2000), Trayvon Martin
(2012), Mike Brown (2014), Tamir Rice (2014), and Philando Castile
(2016) saw time in court, they were neither found guilty nor decertified as policemen.[74] Instead they were promoted or transferred; even
those who had been terminated were allowed to continue working
as officers in other counties. The trials that did go forward did more
to prosecute victims than perpetrators, while the wrongful death
suits that followed—which for many was the most readily available
means of compelling accountability—simply quantified black life in
ways reminiscent of the auction block.[75] The historical and successive nature of lynching belies lofty narratives of racial progress to
illustrate how antiblack violence shares a relationship of interiority
with the making and maintenance of the nation and its people.

The question "Why lynching, why now?" then, reflects a common
misreading of our contemporary moment, as it implies that lynching is over, that it is a thing of the past, and that this past has no
material or symbolic bearing on the present. This book disturbs such

thinking by illustrating how lynching continues to function rhetorically as a performance of American identity, constitutively as a practice of civic supremacy and citizenship belonging, and epideictically as a kind of racialized civic pedagogy and a blueprint for civic life. The structure of the book seeks to aid this effort. Chapter 1 demonstrates how lynching gained its civic resonance. In this chapter I analyze the rhetoric of governing and landmark legislation in an effort to trace how laws rhetorically constituting "the people" rendered blacks "political enemies" as opposed to "political friends," coded "citizen" and "citizenship" as the sole purview of those with white racial standing, and defined black life as expendable life in ways that configured antiblack violence—specifically, lynching—as a customary performance of white citizenship identity. The aim of this chapter is to illustrate how the rhetorical construction of the "citizen" was "underwritten by a supplemental anti-Blackness"[76] that both informed lynching as a performance of American identity and citizenship belonging.

Chapter 2 continues the discussion of lynching as a performance of American identity and citizenship belonging through attention to the rhetorical power of lynching photographs. In this chapter I use rhetorical theory and analysis to demonstrate how lynching photographs functioned epideictically as lessons in civics and democratic citizenship. Regardless of the communities in which they circulated, lynching photographs retained their resonance as scripts for civic life while equally retaining their cultural and political value as pedagogies of civic belonging. Here my discussion of lynching photographs as models of citizenship is meant to set the stage for later discussion of their utility in present-day battles to both preserve and contest a white democracy. Chapter 3 extends my exploration into the epideictic power of lynching photographs to consider how contemporary circulation of lynching photographs, specifically, the traveling photography collection *Without Sanctuary: Lynching Photographs in America*, contributed to the perpetuation of a critical democratic literacy similar to that outlined by anti-lynching activists of the 1930s. Of additional interest here is how the rhetoric of the collection both cultivates public memory of lynching and encourages attendees to draw continuity between the nation's past and present proclivity for state-sanctioned antiblack violence. At the turn of the twenty-first century, museum and cultural center executives throughout the nation hosting *Without Sanctuary* produced a rhetorical domain in which the memory of lynching was used to provide contemporary citizens an interpretive lens through which to read the state-sanctioned killing of black men by police during the twenty-first century as the continuance of America's tradition of lynching. Such framing, I argue, continues the work of anti-lynching activists and organizations of the early nineteenth century who sought to use images of lynching to cultivate a critical democratic literacy among citizens. Such framing, I argue, contests claims that lynching is dead. As *Without Sanctuary* makes clear, lynching is alive and well.

The final chapters of the book continue to examine the rhetorical culture of lynching through attention to how tropes of lynching are deployed in contemporary political discourse. In Chapter 4 I examine the discourse around lynched effigies of then-senator Barack Obama, which appeared just weeks before Obama secured the 2008 presidential nomination for the Democratic Party. Like their literal counterparts, these mock lynchings blended the practice of constructing an "enemy," affirming the racial composition of the citizenry, and refreshing the spirit of democracy through violent acts of identification and display. Here I give attention to how discourse defending Obama effigies as a constitutional right carried the same rhetorical signature as discourse defending lynching, how such discourse mirrored pro-lynching rhetoric at the turn of the nineteenth century in ways that constructed the presidency—like the citizenry—as a "whites only" designation, and lastly, how the black body in peril continues to figure for citizens across the color line as a symbol of white democracy. In the final chapter I discuss the 2012 iteration of Obama effigies before I return to the 2012 lynching of Trayvon and a discussion of how and why members of the black community interpreted Trayvon's death—and the deaths of so many others—as extensions of American lynching. As many concluded, Trayvon's death belied claims of an America beyond race, to reveal antiblack violence as a changing same of democratic citizenship.

CHAPTER ONE

CONSTITUTING THE "CITIZEN RACE"

*Blacks are the objects of a constitutional omission which has
been incorporated into a theory of neutrality. It is thus that
omission is really a form of expression, as oxymoronic as that
sounds: racial omission is a literal part of original intent; it is
the fixed, reiterated prophecy of the Founding Fathers.*
—PATRICIA WILLIAMS, *Alchemy of Race and Rights*[1]

The aim of rhetorical enterprise, explains Kenneth Burke, is to reduce
dissimilarity, to find ways of demonstrating likeness or sameness
for the purpose of inducing cooperation, building alliances, and
establishing community. This aim is assisted by what Burke refers to
as *rhetorical identification*, a practice in which social actors render
themselves *consubstantial,* or *similar to each other* with the intention of inducing attitude and moving each other to action.[2] Acts of
identification give shape and substance to the imagined community that is "the people." Its role in constituting a social collective,
however, employs language that is inherently divisive. While using
language and other forms of symbolic action to give shape and
substance to an imagined "us," identification simultaneously gives
shape to a "them," against which we—that is, "us"—is constituted.
This is inevitably the other half of Burke's dialectic: to *rhetorically*

identify with one is to *rhetorically disidentify* with another. In the case of nation building, "we the people" is rhetorically constituted through language that distinguishes the existence of an "us" through comparison with, or juxtaposition to, that of an imagined or constructed "them." As the logic goes: "There can be no sense of *us* without a sense of what and who *we* are not, and to determine what and who *we* are not is, at the same time, to determine who *they* ("others") are." Typically referred to as the "us/them" dialectic, this form of social organizing, fostered by acts of identification, is most often employed in the service of political mobilization. Its rhetorical power resides in its ability to establish a definitional profile that, through the act of naming difference or threat, legitimates action against it and, in so doing, enacts the ideological boundaries requisite for social and political collectiveness.

The founding documents, legal provisions, social performances, and language used to articulate American national identity between 1776 and 1870 are directly guided by appeals to sameness that employ narratives of a common past, homogeneity, and religious secularism meant to foster a sense of collectivism among an otherwise nebulous population, and to nurture a definition of civic identity predicated upon ideological beliefs in natural right and racial superiority. In this chapter I discuss how the "us/them" dialectic manifest in the laws governing US citizenship, the behavior used to enact it, and the language employed by those inscribed by it culminated in the racial codification of the American citizen. Laws constituting citizenship were directly guided by appeals to an "us" that figured "the people" as a racially homogeneous group and "them" as a collection of subhuman nonwhite others. In this chapter I demonstrate how legislative appeals to a racially exclusive citizenry coupled with a vested interest in retaining a white racial state instigated conditions that made the lynching of black citizens a revered performance of white citizenship identity. What I hope to trace here is a rhetoric of enemyship[3] that outlines how social actors legislated a white ideal through various ways of racializing the enemy. Chief to this analysis is how founding and landmark legislation mapped an "us/them" dialectic onto appeals to founders' intent to legally codify citizenship as a "whites only" designation, and how this discourse erected a rhetorical border[4] that constructed blacks as antithetical to citizenship, their eventual inclusion within the nation as a perversion of democracy, and their symbolic expulsion through the ritual violence of lynching as a performance of American civic identity.

This chapter is divided into two sections. The first section illustrates how the Declaration of Independence and the U.S. Constitution laid the foundation for a racialized definition of the citizen and how later provisions such as the Naturalization Act of 1790, Compromise of 1820, *Dred Scott* decision, and black codes of 1866 onward further solidified this definition. To clarify, the goal of this section is not to offer an exhaustive overview of the nation's founding documents but rather to illustrate how appeals to sameness by way of rhetorically disidentifying with black humanity undergird laws codifying American civic belonging as a call to white solidarity. I conclude this section with an analysis of how Chief Justice Taney's 1857 opinion in *Dred Scott vs. Sanford*, which legally codified America's "citizen race" as white and male, reinscribed color-line logic through appeals to founders' law and founders' intent.

In the second section I examine antiblack lynching as a performance of American identity, one that construes citizenship belonging along racial lines. Rituals of citizenship belonging range from benign acts such as voting and observing the law to ritualistic performances of depravity and racialized violence such as lynching. Of particular importance to this section is how one's sense of "place" within the polity is rhetorically constituted through lynching and customary acts of display and spectatorship associated with the practice. This chapter's consideration of the racist constitution of "the citizen" in conjunction with everyday performances of citizenship identity manifest in antiblack violence sets the scene for the book's larger consideration of how lynching functions as an argument against the inclusion of blacks within the nation.

We, the White People

Founding documents, declarations, and legal codes governing citizenship are indexes of motive in that they outline the desires and intentions of the communities they constitute. Legislation outlining the perimeters of citizenship belonging detail a motivational grammar that distinguishes the existence of an "us" through comparison with or juxtaposition to that of a constructed "them." This "us/them" dialectic names the "other" or "enemy" through a combination of contrastive couplings that casts "us"—that is, "the people"—as imbued with the requisite criteria for citizenship, and "them"—nonwhite "others"—as the anticitizen, whose exclusion from the polity both "threatened and consolidated" its status as a white habitus. In 1776 Jefferson employed this dialectic to rhetorically construct Americans as "one people" driven by reason, united by an inalienable right to freedom, and directed by a deft opposition to tyranny.

> When in the Course of human events it becomes necessary for one people to dissolve the political bands which have connected them with another and to assume among the powers of the earth, the separate and equal station to which the Laws of Nature and of Nature's God entitle them, a decent respect to the opinions of mankind requires that they should declare the causes which impel them to the separation.
>
> We hold these truths to be self-evident, that all men are created equal, that they are endowed by their Creator with certain unalienable Rights, that among these are Life, Liberty and the pursuit of Happiness.—That to secure these rights, Governments are instituted among Men, deriving their just powers from the consent of the governed,—That whenever any Form of Government becomes destructive of these ends, it is the Right of the People to alter or to abolish it, and to institute new Government, laying its foundation on such principles and organizing its powers in such form, as to them shall seem most likely to effect their Safety and Happiness . . . But when a long

train of abuses and usurpations, pursuing invariably the same Object evinces a design to reduce them under absolute Despotism, it is their right, it is their duty, to throw off such Government, and to provide new Guards for their future security.—Such has been the patient sufferance of these Colonies; and such is now the necessity, which constrains them to alter their former Systems of Government. The history of the present King of Great Britain is a history of repeated injuries and usurpations, all having in direct object the establishment of an absolute Tyranny over these States.[5]

These first passages declaring "Life, Liberty and the pursuit of Happiness" as the natural and "unalienable rights" of man, situate "the people" as a reason-driven collective, who, in comparison to the unreasonable tyrannous British king, are guided by virtue and a law of natural rights. As such, the web of juxtapositions including *one people: another, citizen: subject, American: British*, and *natural: unnatural* constructing Britain as the "enemy" against which Americans must defend, positioned revolution as a necessary and inevitable consequence of British despotism while figuring "the people" as a political collective constituted by a shared desire for freedom and a readiness to protect it.

Jefferson's figuration of "the people" as inherently free influenced later legislation codifying citizenship as an exclusively white designation. At the 1787 Philadelphia Convention, state representatives hammered out questions over citizenship via debates over slavery. Of issue was how to count state populations so as to determine their representation in Congress. Northern delegates feared that counting slaves as part of these populations would result in a southern-dominated legislature.[6] Also at stake was the possibility of secession; southern delegates refused to enter the Union unless northerners agreed to secure slavery as the constitutional right of white men.[7] While the resulting Three-Fifths Compromise defining slaves as "three-fifths of all other persons"[8] securing southern and northern interests, clarified the civic status of America's slave population, it left the civic status of black freepersons unaddressed. The Naturalization Act of 1790 granting citizenship to nonblack immigrants offered a partial remedy to the issue. While the primary intent of the statute was to secure the allegiance of European immigrants who came to America in search of labor opportunities, its secondary was to more clearly define the color of citizenship.

> ... any Alien *being a free white person*, who shall have resided within the limits and under the jurisdiction of the United States for the term of two years, may be admitted to become a citizen thereof on application to any common law Court of record in any one of the States wherein he shall have resided for the term of one year at least.[9]

While the racist rhetoric of the statute narrowed the constitutional loophole created by the Three-Fifths Compromise, it failed to address the condition of free native-born blacks because it presupposed that native-born individuals were already national citizens on account that they were neither alien nor slave. So, while the law solidified white as the color of federal citizenship, it did nothing to address the fact that US federalism endowed states with the power to grant or deny citizenship to whom they pleased.[10] This discretionary power to bestow or deny civic status produced a black constituency that enjoyed varying degrees of citizenship. For instance, in parts of New England where the free black population was low, blacks were given voting rights; in areas of the mid-Atlantic region, propertied blacks both voted and served on juries.[11]

At the same time, though, because state jurisdiction ceased beyond state boundaries, states unsupportive of black citizenship were under no obligation to recognize or honor the civic liberties granted free blacks by other states. Rejecting black citizenship were states like Pennsylvania and Ohio, which outright denied freepersons residence, and states like Maryland, Tennessee, and North Carolina, which recognized black citizenship but later came to revoke it.[12] State laws ignoring, denying, curbing, and outright revoking the citizenship rights of black freepersons worked to geographically ensure the separation of slaves and free blacks. White racial logic reckoned freepersons a threat because they infected slaves with the spirit of freedom. Establishing geographical barriers to divide these populations, then, was tactical in that it sought to ward off insurgency. Planned revolts led by Haiti's Toussaint Louverture (1791), South Carolina's Denmark Vesey (1822), and Virginia's Nat Turner (1831) provided further impetus for white America's suspicion of free blacks, their assumed ability to influence black slaves, and the ever-constant need to monitor and police the movements of both. As one South Carolinian put it, all blacks

> should be watched with an eye of steady and unremitted observation, … Let it never be forgotten, that our Negroes are freely the JACOBINS of the country; that they are the ANARCHISTS and the DOMESTIC ENEMY: the COMMON ENEMY OF CIVILIZED SOCIETY, and the BARBARIANS WHO WOULD, IF THEY COULD, BECOME THE DESTROYERS OF OUR RACE. [13]

Here a rhetoric of enemyship similar to rhetoric employed by Jefferson to distinguish "the people" from Britain is utilized to distinguish "Negroes" from "OUR [WHITE] RACE." Rhetorically juxtaposing "Jacobin," which denotes a political extremist or rebel, and "civil society," which within the context of the statement figures American whites as potential victims of ill-intending Negroes, crafts a vision of national community through ardent appeals to white solidarity and violent collective action against a black foe. Such discourse races patriotism white and antiblack, while politically charged terminology like "Jacobins," "Anarchists," and "domestic enemy" politicizes "our Negroes" as America's internal "enemy." The juxtaposition of "civilized society" and "destroyers [read: "blacks"]" further exaggerates this claim by stressing dissimilarity to legitimate the use of violent force.

Rhetorically figuring blacks as the enemy within continued as legislators worked to more clearly define citizenship as a "whites only" category. The landmark decision of the *Dred Scott* case illustrates this best through its intent to settle mounting concerns over the color of democratic citizenship. In 1857 a slave named Dred Scott sued in both the state and federal courts of Missouri for recognition as an emancipated, native-born black man. Scott had been the slave of John Emerson, a US Army surgeon, and accompanied him on several trips from the slave state of Missouri to the free state of Illinois and the free territory of Wisconsin. His first suit in 1846 was brought against Irene Emerson, the widow of John Emerson and inheritor of Scott after the death of her husband. Scott's counsel successfully argued that his two-year residence in Illinois and four-year residence in the Wisconsin territory made him free; however, this decision was later overturned in 1852 following the Fugitive Slave Act of 1850 and precedent set in *Strader v. Graham* (1851). *Strader v. Graham* reiterated the Fugitive Slave Act in that it nullified the power of free states to grant freedom to slaves who had relocated to free states or territories. The slave law itself, which also targeted free blacks,[14] was essentially a federal permit authorizing slave masters and white citizens to pursue and seize runaways even after they had crossed into free territory. As the law of the land, the Fugitive Slave Act, then, not only forced free states to concede to the jurisdictional power of slave states even as they operated beyond the boundaries of their own regions, but also made the profiling, surveilling, policing, and seizing of blacks by whites a mandated practice of white citizenship. In 1853 Scott tried again to gain his freedom by suing Irene Emerson's brother, John Sanford, who had purchased him in 1852, but Scott again lost. Following the jurisdiction laws decided in *Strader v. Graham* (1851) and the precedent set in *Scott v. Emerson* (1852), the US circuit court sided with Sanford on the basis that Scott's previous and current residence in Missouri made him a slave.

While a debate over states' rights and state jurisdiction was central to the concluding decisions in *Strader v. Graham* (1851) and *Scott v. Emerson* (1852), they were not the reigning concerns occupying justices when the case reached the Supreme Court in 1857. Of chief concern instead was the political status of America's enslaved, emancipated, and freeborn black populations. Forwarding a traditionalist interpretation of the Declaration and Constitution that cited slavery as the constitutional right of white men, Chief Justice Roger Taney concluded that blacks were not and never could be citizens—that is, one of "us"—because Founding Fathers had deemed them inherently inferior and, thus, "unfit to associate with the white race, either in social or political relations; and so far inferior, that they had no rights which the white man was bound to respect."[15] Who founders conceived to be "the people," he continued, was evidenced by the Constitution, which had drawn a clear "line of division . . . between the *citizen race,* who formed and held the government, and the *African race, which they held in subjection and slavery, and governed at their own pleasure.*" Scott's lawsuit was therefore moot, because he was not and never could be a citizen. Because the founders had conceived of blacks as chattel and thus "persons" excused from the protections of the Constitution, they had, by design "no rights which the white man was bound to respect." [16] Taney's majority ruling utilized an unambiguously racist rhetoric that nullified future petitions for black citizenship by rendering blackness the antithesis of citizenship, "the people" synonymous with "white," and "white" synonymous with the "citizen race." Such discursive bordering, explained one critic, illustrated that Americans were not "entitled to liberty . . . because of abstract ideals of universal human freedom, but rather by virtue of being white."[17]

Reconstituting "Us": Contesting the Polity's Recomposition

If the *Dred Scott* decision of 1857 helped to solidify a white democracy, then the Civil War and subsequent Reconstruction period marked the onset of its demise. The Thirteenth Amendment (1865) abolishing slavery and with it the black "domestic enemy"; the Fourteenth Amendment (1868), transforming black anticitizens into citizens and prohibiting states from denying due process of law; and the Fifteenth Amendment (1870), vesting blacks with the right to vote, disrupted the color-line logic of American citizenship in ways that caused state legislatures of the citizen race to pass a series of explicitly discriminatory laws rooted in the slave codes of the eighteenth and nineteenth centuries.[18] The first laws depriving blacks of their newly endowed constitutional rights were known as the black codes of 1865. Black codes, which defined the rights of ex-slaves, functioned as an immediate juridical counter to abolition and as a strategic means of racializing constitutional protections and citizenship rights as the exclusive protections and rights of those with white racial standing. Black codes denied blacks the right to vote and serve on juries, policed the physical movement of blacks, and ensured black deference to white supremacy through punitive laws that covered everything from presumed idleness, disrespectful conduct, and insulting language to preaching without a license, vagrancy, and labor contracts.[19] The black codes were essentially slave laws in all but name and as such served as a first line of defense against what southern legislators felt was the dismantling of America's civic order. In Mississippi, black codes legislated the searching of black citizens each January for proof of employment. Those without a labor contract at the start of the New Year were considered vagrants and subject to monetary fines and involuntary plantation labor. Those with labor contracts who at times disputed them (because most contracts mandated laborers to work a slaves' shift of sunup to sundown) were often found in violation and subjected to punishment. In Florida, laborers who interrupted their contracts in protest against such abuses suffered forfeiture of wages and arrest by "any white citizen."[20] In Virginia, black workers accused of breaking their labor contracts were whipped, humiliated, and forced to work for free for up to a year. Other states extorted black labor even more assertively. In South Carolina the only means to avoid work as a tenant farmer or servant was to pay an annual tax that ranged anywhere from ten dollars to one hundred.[21]

Black codes defined the rights of black children as well. Those whose parents were unable to care for them (often because they were serving time under vagrancy laws) were contracted out to whites—typically former masters—under apprenticeship laws where, rather than learning a trade, children became servants and field hands. Parental consent was not required, and in many cases parents were completely unaware that the courts had bound their children to white employers.[22] Most important, however, is how black codes defined any act of black self-sufficiency or self-determinacy as an infringement upon the law. During slavery, blacks were free to hunt and fish. However, in the wake of enfranchisement, white legislators considered hunting and other forms of subsistence employed by blacks fertile ground for insurgency. To combat their independence, states such as Virginia, North Carolina, South Carolina, and Georgia created trespassing laws and hunting restrictions in counties with large black populations and imposed taxes on blacks who owned guns or dogs.[23] State laws such as those that denied blacks the capacity to own or rent property, to subsist independent of white interference, and to arm themselves in defense against harm illustrated a concerted effort among white legislators to restore a system of social control that functioned like "slavery in all but its name."[24] Restoring the line delineating America's white "us" from its nonwhite "them" served as a primary means of making the domination of blacks more manageable as the reality of their citizenship became more permanent.[25]

The Civil Rights Act of 1866, which granted citizenship to ex-slaves and endowed them with the same rights enjoyed by whites, was a critical rejoinder to the Black Codes, adamantly opposed by proponents of white democracy.[26] Congressional debate over black citizenship turned on claims of racial degradation that reflected a proclivity to see blacks as perversions of the Constitution.[27] Echoing Taney's appeal to a white racial state, Sen. Thomas Hendricks (D) contended that America was "a white man's Government, made by the white man for the white man" and, on that founding strength alone, should "remain a political community of white people."[28] To do otherwise, he reasoned, would be to undermine the original intent of democratic promise. Reiterating these appeals, New York senator John Winthrop Chanler, who regularly described the United States as a "white democracy," contended that including "the negro race" as part of "'the people'" "pervert[ed] the intention of the framers of the Constitution" and "violate[d] the whole spirit of the preamble."[29] President Johnson demonstrated his support for these attitudes when he vetoed the bill. His veto was in part an appeal to founders' intent that conflated tropes of the mimicking ape with tropes of the black beast to not simply figure blacks as "unfit" for citizenship, but to more devastatingly figure blacks as enemies of the state. He reasoned that blacks were a national threat because they lacked an understanding of what it meant to vote on account that they were "so utterly ignorant of public affairs that their voting [consisted] of nothing more than carrying a ballot to the place where they are directed to deposit it."[30] Johnson's paternalistic entreaty for white Americans to maintain the "national" order of things concluded with an appeal to "states' rights" that dovetailed with Taney's "whites only" vision of "the people." It followed, then, that the push for black suffrage, which according to Johnson was a "privilege" blacks had never before sought or asked for, was a Republican plot to implement "Negro Rule."[31] Such propaganda posited suffrage and increased participation of blacks in government as a direct threat to democracy. Political cartoons perpetuating this logic used tropes of the black threat and the black beast rapist to impress a sense of foreboding doom upon whites. Such propaganda depicted America's new constituency as devils and vampires that fed off innocent and vulnerable citizens of the polity. Other cartoons such as "Remember!" sexualized Negro Rule by personifying America as a white woman shackled to a "Negro Rule" iron ball.[32] Like these images, Johnson's fearmongering rhetoric sought legislation that secured the civic supremacy of whites over blacks[33] through discourse rendering blacks a scourge to the nation.

Figure 1.1. The Vampire That Hovers over North Carolina. News and Observer (Raleigh, NC), September 27, 1898. Courtesy of UNC Libraries, The 1898 Election in North Carolina.

Although white anxiety over the color of elected leadership was prevalent, at no point did blacks ever hold political dominance throughout the region. Among the southern state conventions of 1867–68, blacks on average constituted no more than 26 percent of state legislatures; South Carolina's 61 percent black membership and Louisiana's 50 percent black membership were the only states without a white majority in their conventions.[34] Still, fearmongering from opposition encouraged hostility against blacks in government. In Georgia expulsion of black members of the state legislature came quickly after the removal of federal troops and the state's initial readmission to the Union in 1868.[35] Thirty black members in all were removed on bogus charges of personal misconduct, and in September of that same year were officially declared ineligible to sit as members of the Georgia legislature. The expelled members and white Republicans took the matter to Governor Bullock, who drafted a letter to Congress that asserted the illegitimacy of Georgia's Democrat-dominated house. As he contended, the legislature formed after the expulsion of its black members had been ille-

On the 8th of November these shackles will be broken.

Figure 1.2. Remember! News and Observer (Raleigh, NC), November 3, 1898. Courtesy of UNC Libraries, The 1898 Election in North Carolina.

gally constituted. Congress's decision to intervene on behalf of the expelled members, however, occurred only after the state rejected the Fifteenth Amendment, at which point Georgia was put under the military purview of General Terry, who, after ousting twenty-four Democrats and replacing them with Republicans, reinstated the expelled black members. Georgia remained under military rule until it ratified the Fifteenth Amendment.[36] Despite restoring justice to the expelled legislators, their expulsion as well as the measures taken by Democrats to interrupt progress toward black suffrage was a strong indication of the general anxiety whites experienced over the inclusion of blacks within the nation.

A Rhetoric of Civic Belonging

Reconstruction was a radical refutation of customary attitudes and practices toward blacks, and a challenge to over two hundred years of tradition, conventions, and laws codifying civic identity as white and civic order as a racial order. Laws coercing free black labor, regulations restricting the economic opportunities and constitutional rights of black citizens, and parliamentary actions banning black legislators from government enacted a logic of exclusion that soothed white anxiety over the perceived "blackening" of America. Blacks were no longer the constitutive outside of "the people" but now one of "us," and while refutation of radical Reconstruction manifested as law curtailing the constitutional rights of blacks, and more specifically as the expulsion of blacks from various levels of the legislature, in the cities and towns of the everyday citizen, rejecting the recomposition of "the people" manifested as an early American ritual of political affiliation. Whereas lynch law during the American Revolution constituted the nation through the expulsion of Tories, lynch law during American Reconstruction sought to secure the nation through the expulsion of blacks. Like the Constitution,

Naturalization Act of 1790, and black codes, lynching enacted an epistemological view of civic order as racial order that figured blacks as antithetical to citizenship, and lynching as a symbolic means of reconstituting "the people" as Taney's "citizen race." Annulling the constitutional rights of blacks through spectacular disavowal of those rights, then, was a communicative act that reflected who "the people" imagined themselves to be. As such, it was a violent act of nation making that prompted members of the citizenry to rhetorically identify with one another through a collective and spectacular disavowal of black citizenship rights and black humanity.

Over 4,500 individuals were lynched between 1882 and 1968 alone, the majority of whom—a recorded 3,220—were African American men.[37] Long-held imaginings regarding the "inherent" immorality and barbarity of blacks helped to legitimate lynching while simultaneously concealing the various social, economic, and political factors that contributed to its practice. Reconstruction led to greater competition over work, the increased economic independence of blacks, black political activism, and the erosion of customary performances of black deference.[38] Failure to perform the customary routine of black acquiescence to white dominance was met with violence. For instance, in 1888 black sharecroppers Tom Smith and John Coleman met their end as a result of what historian William Fitzhugh Brundage calls "insufficient subservience."[39] As Brundage explains, Smith and Coleman's decision to take their cotton first to their supplier, rather than their employer, transgressed codes of racial etiquette that resulted in their deaths; customarily planters received first claim to sharecroppers' harvest. Enraged, the men's employer sought a warrant for their arrest, but Smith and Coleman refused to be taken. Instead, they went to their supplier, secured weaponry, and fought capture by the posse that eventually overtook them and lynched them. Rather than stringing Smith and Coleman to a tree, the posse improvised by tying rocks around their necks and throwing the two men into the river.[40] Insufficient subservience and insolence to the racial order also took the form of expressed condemnation over the unjust treatment of blacks. In 1919 Ernest Glenwood was lynched for "trying to organize black workers to refuse to work for 60 cents a day." After the triple lynching of three black men near Leesburg, Georgia, Enoch Daniels, a black resident who had been warned several times for publically denouncing the triple lynching, was taken from his home by a group of white men and hanged.[41] In these instances, lynching sought to "right" or "correct" what whites had deemed transgressions to the racial order.

The most common justifications for lynchings were murder, rape, and attempted rape. These three accusations alone culminated in the lynching of 3,137 people (66.4 percent of the total individuals lynched) from 1882 to 1968.[42] In Georgia 205 blacks were lynched under the charge of murder, and 124 for alleged rape. Numbers in Virginia, conversely, were significantly lower: thirty-one individuals were lynched for murder, while only thirty-three were lynched for rape.[43] The conditions under which these alleged offenses occurred, however, were often precarious in nature. Frequently in instances of murder, black men were not outwardly seeking to kill but were instead defending themselves, families, and property from the malicious objectives of ill-intentioned whites. In 1892 Thomas Moss, Calvin McDowell, and Henry Stewart were lynched when an attempt on their Memphis grocery store, the People's Grocery Company, ended in the wounding of three white men. The People's Grocery Company was a black-owned and black-operated business that served residents of "the Curve," a black neighborhood in Memphis named for its location along the sharp bend of the streetcar line. People's Grocery posed a threat to the white-owned Barrett's grocery, which had served the area for some time. Resentment over the three men's growing monopoly of black clientele turned violent when a fight broke out between a black boy and a white boy playing marbles near the two stores. After being bested in the game, the white boy sought his father, a man named Hurst, who then whipped the black boy in retaliation. When black men in the area heard about the incident, they rallied together and approached Hurst. Barrett, who was close by, came to Hurst's defense and swore revenge against the men, among whom the owners of People's Grocery included.[44] On August 11, Barrett's attempt to make good on his threat was thwarted when armed white men entering the rear of People's Grocery were shot. After the incident local authorities arrested and charged Moss, McDowell, and Stewart. The three sat in jail under the watchful eye of black citizens until on the third day, after fear of lynching had subsided, they were left alone. Shortly thereafter, the three men were removed from their cells, taken to the outskirts of town, and riddled with bullets.[45] A similar incident occurred in 1901 when Sterling Thompson, a successful black farmer and political activist living in Campbellton, Georgia, was killed while defending his estate against white moonshiners who resented not only his efforts to shut down their stills but also his economic prosperity.[46]

Accusations of rape, on the other hand, entailed a different array of circumstances. As Sandy Alexandre explains, white women's bodies were "marked territory" in lynching discourse. Rhetorically constructed as "no-trespassing zones," white women's bodies "symbolized the plenitude of white superiority" and therefore "the most precious form" of white space and white property. While institutionalized slavery and the dehumanization of black bodies made the systematic rape of black women acceptable, the rape of white women (whether real or imagined) was deemed deplorable, unpardonable, and punishable by death.[47] As a result, black men accused of raping white women swiftly fell under full force of lynch law. Notions of southern gentility intertwined with Victorian norms of feminine virtue and masculine valor categorized the lynching of alleged black rapists as the work of "leading citizens." Following these conventions, white supremacist supporters and lynching apologists rationalized lynching as a kind of necessary evil, one committed by a community of citizens who logically sought retribution against black brutality. For instance, the 1930 lynching of James Irwin of Irwin County, Georgia, was explained by advocates and apologists as a necessary, just, and rationale outcome to the alleged rape of a young white girl.

Irwin's lynching garnered a decent amount of criticism. Many were surprised when news broke of the lynching, as Irwin "bore a good reputation" in the community and was described as a "well-behaved Negro" and "hardworking field hand."[48] Additionally, Georgia had been lynching-free for the past three years, and some residents felt that Irwin's lynching and the local weekly's announced support created "unfavorable publicity" for the state.[49] An editorial retort illustrates Alexandre's point in the way it metonymically figured the honor of white women as the sacrosanct space of the white community.

Some of those who have criticised us most severely for the lynching that occurred in our county last Saturday seem to have almost lost sight of the fact that a most heinous crime had been committed the afternoon before by the man who was lynched. They lose sight of the fact that one of our *pure lovely young girls just budding into attractive young womanhood was attacked and slain by the wanton brute who was the victim of the mob's summary punishment.* . . . It is one thing to sit behind a mahogany desk a hundred miles away when one knows nothing of the persons concerned and write scathing editorials on the abstract subject of lynching and its evils. It is quite another thing when it comes close home to us as did last Friday's crime. When it is some other man's daughter or wife, especially if he is far removed from the *moralizer,* it is easy to see what ought not to have been done. When it is one's own wife or daughter or the wife or daughter of a one's neighbor, it is quite a different matter. . . . This paper does not condone lynching, but *so long as this crime is committed, so long can criminals expect mob violence.* . . . Let us all hope that there will never be another lynching in Irwin County and that there will be no crime like the one that caused this one.[50]

Juxtapositions such as "pure lovely girl" and "wonton brute" recast the epic struggle between good and evil as the ongoing battle to protect white purity from the taint of black wickedness. As the paper's editor illustrates, apologists rationalized lynching as righteous action that would end only when the sensibilities of civilized people ceased to be offended by the imagined rapaciousness of black brutes.

The editor's melodramatic retort exemplifies how appeals to lynching rhetorically defined democratic citizenship by setting the terms of belonging. For instance, language linking the white female victim with the community metonymically constructed the lynching audience as "the people" and the "delicate virtue" of white womanhood as the body politic. And while the conventions of Victorian mores keep the editor from explicitly describing the crime, words like "young" and "budding," which allude to the violation of a ripening sexuality imagined to be the exclusive property of white men, situated antimiscegenation as a fundamental term of belonging. If you understood the dire need to protect white womanhood and the white community, if you understood the importance of civility and safety, then you belonged; if you did not, if you contested Irwin's lynching or read the actions residents took as rash and indecent, then you did not belong. To live and be a citizen of the Irwin community, then, was to either implicitly or explicitly consent to lynching James Irwin. This rhetorical construction of citizenship belonging, as Ashraf Rushdy points out, was also gendered male. Lynching Irwin was about crime and punishment as much as it was about "masculine honor—the right to protect heart, home, and family." Those who failed to "appreciate that imperative," the editor implied, were not citizens of the community.[51]

While the editor reminded readers that the weekly did not endorse lynching, his counter to the criticism produced a justification for lynching that was classically apologist in the way it rationalized lynching as an "unfortunate" but understandable response to the violation of white women and the nation, painted lynchers as virtuous civil citizens, and figured lynching victims as brutes deserving of violent exclusion from the society. Such discourse rhetorically situating lynchings as a consequence of black debauchery worked to combat accusations of white barbarity by casting blacks as morally unfit for civil society. The myth of white feminine virtue aided this logic by reasoning that white women would never willingly engage in interracial sex. However, as Wells's investigative reporting revealed, it was more common than not for lynching victims accused of rape to be the lovers of their accusers or the lovers of the women they were accused to have violated.[52] Such findings led Wells to unequivocally assert, "Nobody in this section of the country believes the old thread-bare lie that Negro men rape white women. If Southern white men are not careful," she continued, "they will over-reach themselves, and public sentiment will have a reaction; a conclusion will then be reached which will be very damaging to the moral reputation of their women."[53] A 1940s survey of antimiscegenation laws and interracial marriages echoes Wells's point. Laws criminalizing various forms of interracial mixing had been in circulation since 1822. Researchers studying interracial relations between 1916 and 1937 found that out of the 3,131 mixed-raced marriages surveyed, four-fifths of them were between black men and white women.[54] To be sure, laws criminalizing interracial relations, interracial cohabitation, and interracial marriage were more a means of policing the private interactions of black men and white women than those of blacks and whites in general. As a result, these laws had little bearing on the sexual exploits of white men who since slavery had enjoyed access to the sexual rights of both black and white women. Miscegenation laws, then, more than anything else, were a means of marking the sexual, reproductive, and property rights of white women as the exclusive purview of white men. Lynching was its performative corollary.

Reconstituting the "Citizen Race"

Lynchings reaffirmed communal spirit in the face of major social change. Like members of federal and state legislatures, members of the white lay public found the civic status of blacks troubling. The growing economic independence of blacks, black political activism, and the erosion of customary modes of black deference[55] contributed to white anxiety over the perceived "blackening" of the polity and the ability to maintain the privileges of citizenship as the exclusive rights of those with white racial standing. In cities and towns, rejection of the Civil War Amendments manifested as a violent ritual of political affiliation in which the torture and hanging of black citizens by their white counterparts replaced legislators' seemingly more "diplomatic" use of laws, court decisions, congressional petitions, and senate expulsions to maintain the racial integrity of the polity.

"Mob citizenship," as Leighweis-Goff describes it, enacted the "rhetorical disembodiment"[56] of blacks from the category "citizen." At the heart of lynching was a fundamental disavowal of black humanity and black citizenship—"I am not that! That is not me!" More aptly put, lynchings were occasions that invited whites to rhetorically identify with one another while rhetorically disidentifying with the abject figure of the soon-to-be-lynched black citizen. As Greg Clark reminds, public experience that prompts "individuals to choose with whom they will identify themselves and with whom they will not . . . constitutes much of what they experience as identity."[57] At lynchings, men, women, and children stood together as a collective body of citizens united through their conformity to the myth of white racial dominance and black inferiority, their acceptance of the assumed guilt of the accused, and their sanctioning of the community's decision to rescind the civic rights of the victim through blood sacrifice and communal celebration. These rhetorical enactments of citizenship communicated who lynchers believed themselves to be relative to blacks and at the same time served as performances of white solidarity that fortified the racial status quo. In this way lynching became the performance of a racialized civic identity, the focal point of reenacted citizenship participation that pointed back to America's founding, Judge Lynch, and violence in defense of the nation and "the people."

Efforts to depict lynching as the lawful expression of "the people" also included the strategic use of land. The selection of highly trafficked, highly public spaces such as courthouse lawns, jailhouse grounds, and town squares placed lynching spectacles at the center of civic life. Such spaces symbolized bureaucratic order, represented the system of checks and balances intended to secure the rights and privileges of "the people," and reiterated the logic of white democracy in that they were regularly the site of slave auctions and public floggings. As representations of both state and federal systems of government and as the backdrop of many lynching spectacles, town centers imparted an air of authority and legislative legitimacy upon lynchers and lynching.[58] The federal government's refusal to intervene on behalf of its black citizenry helped to further legitimate lynching as the venerable practice of America's "leading citizens."

The lynched black body functioned as a powerfully persuasive symbol of antiblack citizenship. Lynched black bodies adorned with rope and chain-linked nooses, riddled with bullets, dismembered, and burned were paraded through town streets, displayed at town centers, left to swing on jail and courthouse lawns, and dragged through black communities. Such public displays at seats of civic life "drew clearly defined ideological and spatial lines" demarcating America's white "us" from its black "them."[59] News reports describing the pro-lynching public as a collection of the "best," "leading," and most respectable citizens, and the lynching victim as a black beast threat compounded this identification by framing antiblack violence as civic duty and lynchers as loyal members of the polity united in their efforts to safeguard the nation from penetrating blackness.[60] Transforming the black citizen into the lynching victim was, then, an act of communion and display that marked lynching as "the doing" of citizenship.

Conclusion

Lynching was a rhetorically constitutive act reconstituting the original designation of the "citizen race" and, along with it, the liberties associated with Americanness as the exclusive purview of whites. As documents like the Constitution, the Naturalization Act of 1790, and landmark decisions like *Dred Scott* made clear, the rhetorical construction and legal codification of "the people" as a political body endowed with unalienable rights and privileges consonant with human subjectivity rendered white racial standing synonymous with citizenship, civic space as space for "whites only," and the constitutive outside of American civic belonging as the dark space of the nonwhite, black "other." Between 1901 and 1934, numerous attempts to pass federal anti-lynching legislation failed because Congress contended, following white separatists and lynching apologists, that such bills violated states' rights. Although some states created laws against lynching and worked to prosecute offenders, the communal dynamic present within local towns often protected lynchers from being prosecuted.[61] Even in the face of photographic evidence, eyewitness testimony, and personal confessions, coroners' reports commonly concluded that lynching victims died at the "hands of persons unknown."[62]

Communicating who and what we are to one another through acts of collective violence is a rhetorical enterprise intended to forge and maintain alliances, create and sustain community, and direct future action. The constitutive power of lynching situates it as a shared moment of identity negotiation that, as Greg Clark reminds, is the "stuff" of civic life.[63] Through their violent performance of dis-identifying with the humanity and civic status of the black citizen, the white citizen race reconstituted its sense of collective identity and, along with it, its political standing as the ultimate citizen. Lynch law, then, which mirrored governing legislation mapping the racially prescribed place of blacks relative to that of "the people," was more than a collective statement against the inclusion of blacks within the polity. Lynch law was a rhetorical enactment that reconstructed democratic citizenship itself.

CHAPTER TWO

A LESSON IN CIVICS

The figures in the photographs had never seemed to have been alive, but were more like signs or symbols one found on the last pages of the dictionary.

—RALPH ELLISON, *Invisible Man*[1]

In Chapter 1 I discuss lynching as a rhetorical performance that enacted the color-line logic of American civic belonging as outlined by governing documents. Lynching materializes an ideological belief that endorsed "the charred and beaten body of a black man hanging by his neck from a tree limb [as] the synecdochal image of the post-Reconstruction condition of the freeedperson."[2] As a form of violent symbolic action tied to founders' racialized notion of "the people," lynching functioned as a counterargument to the inclusion of blacks within the nation and at the same time as a violent performance of white citizenship and white nation making. In this chapter I build upon this premise by turning attention to the epideictic power of lynching imagery and the iconic image of the lynching victim. While once conceived as a mode devoid of social or political utility,[3] epideictic rhetoric as treated here follows the conceptual arc of contemporary scholars of rhetoric and communication who assert its didactic and educative function.[4] Lynching imagery is a form of political iconography that inculcates citizens to the practice of white democracy by way of modeling antiblack violence as a customary, natural, and, revered practice of white civic identity.[5] As such, it provided citizens along the color line with a kind of civic education that imparted crucial knowledge about the practice of American democracy from the 1880s onward. Proponents of the citizen race and anti-lynching activists each circulated images of lynching as paradigmatic examples of democratic citizenship.

In what follows I consider how images of lynching used to both promote and denounce lynching imparted crucial knowledge about civic life and functioned epideictically for citizens as lessons in civics. My attention here to how images of lynching circulated as emblems of white citizenship and American identity grounds my later discussion of how images and news of modern-day lynchings such as those of Trayvon Martin, Tamir Rice, and Michael Brown, among others, and creative adaptions to the lynching tradition such as the chair lynchings of 2008 and 2012, produced rhetorical outcomes similar to those of the nineteenth and twentieth centuries.

Images of Reputable Citizenship

Epideictic rhetoric is largely understood as a response to communal exigencies and is commonly referred to as "a rhetoric of display" or a "praise and blame" in that it "displays what is worthy of praise and narrates the example as a contemporary point of reference."[6] It is a form of address that commonly marks ceremonial occasions in which the virtues and vices of an individual, object, or institution are publically displayed and evaluated before an audience for the purpose of informing and directing future behavior. This orientation toward the future highlights the didactic nature of epideictic rhetoric. As rhetoricians Chaim Perelman and Lucie Olbrechts-Tyteca contend, the educative force of epideictic rhetoric originates from its presumption of community and promotion of values the rhetor envisions shared by members of that imagined community.[7] Following Christine Oravec, John C. Adams affirms that such acts of display function as paradigmatic examples of excellence[8] and thus as didactic scenes in which citizens are taught or in some cases reminded of the chief principles of collective belonging and encouraged to adopt or renew their commitment to them. Such displays serve as lessons for how to enact collective identity.

Scholars working at the intersection of visual cultural studies and rhetoric contend similarly for visual epideictic what rhetoric and communication scholars contend for epideictic speech, namely, that visual images likewise function as didactic modes of display that inculcate viewers to the values, principles, and beliefs of a collective identity.[9] This is in part what Robert Hariman and John Louis Lucaites, echoing insights from Danielle Allen, contend for political iconography. As they explain, iconic images relay ideological codes that "offer performative guides" for what it means to be a member of the polity.[10] Images of lynching were instructive in this way. Like all iconic images, lynching photographs reproduced dominant ideology and communicated social knowledge that instructed citizens in the "ordinary habits" and "deep rules" of democratic citizenship.[11] Within this context, photographs of a degraded black body flanked by crowds of smiling white faces depicted the contract of racial exploitation and eradication that secured democratic promise.[12] Thus, if the lynching spectacle demonstrated the practices of civic life during postemancipation America, then the lynching photograph, by way of its resonance as an irrefutable representation of "the real," ideologically naturalized lynching as an esteemed practice of white citizenship.[13] The naturalizing power of the lynching photograph turned on nineteenth-century empiricist-driven rationales that purported the objectivity of photograph technology. Such logic allowed viewers to assume that photographs were accurate and factual representations of reality rather than reproductions of already-in-place structures of power.[14] The visual rhetoric of the photograph, specifically, the stock image of a mutilated black body juxtaposed with a well-dressed audience of white onlookers, and its circulation within a discourse that rhetorically framed black men as a threat to society, invited viewers to assume the moral integrity of lynchers and the moral depravity of lynching victims.[15] The uniformity of the photographs, specifically how lynchers were portrayed as "stalwart and controlled," while "black victims were portrayed as captive and defiled,"[16] reinforced the very discourse of white civility that legitimated lynching. Under these optics lynchers were interpreted as stately and virtuous citizens who protected the community; under such optics prideful white faces juxtaposed with tattered black bodies evidenced the containment of a "threat" that had plagued America since slavery.

Photographic conventions following seventeenth-century painted portraitures of the hunt contributed to the naturalizing power of pro-lynching photography. Portraiture depicted scenes of piety, gentility, and stateliness and signified the ideological certainty of the aristocracy's superiority over the peasantry. Imagery such as this, which distinguished the cultured from the common, modeled decorum and offered viewers ways of reading their place within the social order. Scenes of the hunt were a common subject of portraiture that figured white men as proper providers and protectors. In lynching photographs, the regal and erudite postures struck by lynchmen, which mirrored those of the respectable aristocrat and gentleman hunter, portrayed lynchers as esteemed members of the citizenry, and lynching victims as quarry to be stalked, trapped, mutilated, and mounted. Such framing helped to normalize and depoliticize lynching by rhetorically framing antiblack violence as a practice of everyday subsistence.[17]

Lynching photographs often depicted a combination of partially clothed, charred, and castrated corpses at times draped with sheets that covered removed genitalia. Stock images of victims in different stages of disarray, nudity, and dismemberment reaffirmed white fantasies as once fully clothed black men were made into the subhuman persons white America had long imagined them to be. Omitting scenes of torture from the photograph helped perpetuate the image of the stately and respectable white citizenry. As Amy Louise Wood notes, choosing to document moments before or after as opposed to during the lynching reinforced the image of "a united and orderly white citizenry in full control and mastery over savage and inhuman black men."[18] Lynching photographs were, thus, staged depictions of white refinement that framed antiblack violence as the work of the "leading" and "best citizens"[19] of the community.

Adapting images of lynching to the postcard tradition spoke to the educative value of lynching imagery at the same time that it revealed the federal government's investment in spreading the gospel of white citizenship.[20] As Robert Hariman and John Louis Lucaites explain, images circulated among a national public serve as epideictic displays of citizenship in that they offer individuals examples of how to enact their identities as members of an imagined community. These didactic scenes of collective identity help citizens come to learn who they are "as private individuals and public citizens by seeing [themselves] reflected in images" and who they "can become by transporting [themselves] into the image."[21] Publicizing his attendance at the 1916 lynching of William Stanley in Temple, Texas, Joe writes: "This is the barbecue we had last night. My picture is to the left with a cross over it. Your sone [sic] Joe."[22] Sending and receiving postcards featuring black abjection juxtaposed with affectionate messages to friends and family granted both white senders and white recipients the opportunity to demonstrate their adherence to a white ideal and their allegiance to a white racial order.[23] As Shawn Michelle Smith notes, sending postcards both performed community and "enlarge[d] community in the same act, for these images symbolically expand[ed] a community's claim on time and space by connecting static individuals to distant places."[24] Joe's circulation of the image alongside his invitation to look on with praise as opposed to disparagement serves a rhetorical constitutive function in that it invited recipients to identify with his role as a member of the "citizen race" by engaging in the process of locating themselves within the image. Such work expanded the pro-lynching public beyond the immediacy of the lynching scene through its invitation to disidentify with the black victim and to identify with white onlookers.[25]

While most images of lynching were sent as commemorative mementos among supporters of and sympathizers with white supremacy, others were sent as threats to those who challenged it. Sending images of lynching to members of the black community reinforced the ideological boundaries originally constituting "the people" at the same time it sought to induce black acquiescence to a white racial order via the ever-constant threat of antiblack violence. In this way, pro-lynching photographs sent to blacks functioned much like the bodies dragged through black communities, hung on the outskirts of black neighborhoods, and positioned along roadways to black schools. Whether an actual body or a visual reproduction, the warning for blacks to stay in their racially prescribed place remained the same.

Depicting an Uncivil Leading Citizenry

The same circulation meant to extend the reach of white supremacist ideology inevitably contributed to the inability to control the signifying power of the lynching photograph. In the hands of anti-lynching proponents, images of black bodies dangling before proud white faces became a means of contesting white imaginings of the nation. Anti-lynching discourse emphasized the contradictions between America's professed ideals and the actuality of their practice by recirculating images of lynching as emblems of white barbarity, and incivility. Ida B. Wells was one of the first to repurpose lynching imagery in this way. In *A Red Record* (1895), Wells supplemented her investigative report of lynching—which included statistics of lynching throughout the nation, catalogued these lynchings by alleged offense, and emphasized the inconsistencies between their rationales and the intent behind their actual practice—with two lynching photographs, those of the 1893 lynchings of C. J. Miller and Lee Walker, both of which appeared in chapters that discussed how innocent black men are scapegoated by lynching-for-rape discourse.[26] Wells's investigation of these two incidents yielded that white officers and white officials exercised a consistent disregard for proof of guilt and due process when it came to black citizens. For instance, while there were several witnesses who testified that C.J. Miller *was not* the man in question, officers detained him, marked him guilty, and permitted the community to lynch him anyway. Rather than lynching Miller with rope, the community placed a hundred-foot metal chain around his neck and body and "led and dragged him through the streets of the village . . . followed by thousands of people" before lynching him, photographing the lynching, and removing his toes and fingers.[27] Lee Walker was lynched for allegedly assaulting two white women who were en route to town. However, when authorities spoke with him a few days later, he explained that he had not assaulted the women but had rather asked them for food. Wells draws attention to this and other inconsistencies regarding Walker's lynching to not only highlight the arbitrariness of the practice, but the fundamentally uncivil nature of America's "leading" and "best citizens." Despite the cited "transgression" there was no evidence that Walker had attacked anyone, and because the cultural logic of lynching excused white women from having to identify alleged assailants, Walker was for all intents and purposes, always already guilty on account of being black. The fact that officials denied Walker the opportunity to corroborate his innocence—the women he was accused of assaulting were never allowed to identify him—signifies on the premeditated nature of his lynching, as does the telegram announcing his lynching, which was released the day before. "Lee Walker, colored man, accused of raping white women, in jail here, will be taken out and burned by whites to-night."[28] The following day Walker was removed from his cell, dragged through town, strung to a telephone pole on Front Street, mutilated, hanged, and finally burned; all this as policemen and deputy sheriffs watched without protest.[29] The crowd's disregard for due process, asserted Wells, refuted claims of white civility by testifying to the moral depravity of not just the white lay public, but the white policemen and sheriffs who by law were charged with securing Walker's rights. Such contradictions, she continued, revealed that lynchings were not impulsive responses to moral outrage, but instead well-organized and well-orchestrated dramas that exposed the concerted effort between everyday citizens and law enforcement to enforce white supremacy. Such a conspiracy, she concluded, was what made lynching a "national crime."

Juxtaposing the image of the black lynching victim with investigative reporting that highlighted these incongruences invited readers to question the presumed guilt of lynching victims, the projected ethos of lynchers, and the discourses of black savagery and white moral authority that legitimated lynching. Deconstructing the logic and discourse of lynching in this way guided Wells' constituency of black citizens and white allies to see victims of lynching as the scapegoats white America needed them to be. It was through epidictic techniques such as these, explains Ashraf Rushdy, that Wells transformed "icons of white pride into emblems of American shame."[30]

Wells herself had originally believed that lynchings were a condition of black depravity until the owners of People's Grocery, with whom she was close, were lynched in Memphis. Her investigation into the lynching at the Curve demonstrated how victims Thomas Moss, Calvin McDowell, and Henry Stewart had been lynched on account of economic competition. People's Grocery had begun to monopolize Barrett's black clientele. The three white men that were later killed during a raid on the People's Grocery, then, were an excuse locals used to justify removing Moss, McDowell, and Stewart from jail and lynching them. Wells' laid the case out clearly,

> The city of Memphis has demonstrated that neither character nor standing avails the Negro if he dares to protect himself against the white man or become his rival. There is nothing we can do about the lynching now, as we are out-numbered and without arms. The white

Figure 2.1. Lynching of C. J. Miller, Bardwell, Kentucky. July 7, 1893.

mob could help itself to ammunition without pay, but the order was rigidly enforced against the selling of guns to Negroes. There is therefore only one thing left that we can do; save our money and leave a town which will neither protect our lives and property, nor give us a fair trial in the courts, but takes us out and murders us in cold blood when accused by white persons.[31]

Within two months of the editorial, six thousand black people left Memphis while those who remained, including Wells, boycotted white businesses.[32] As Wells discovered, lynchings were ordinarily responses to black achievement and consensual relationships between black men and white women as opposed to incidents of crime and rape.[33]

The Hypocrisy of American Democracy

In the hands of anti-lynching activists such as Wells, lynching photography became a rich resource for educating black citizens on the hypocrisy of American democracy. In 1916 *Crisis*, the official news organ for the National Association for the Advancement of Colored People (NAACP), published an article titled "Peonage" that reprinted the image of a Georgia lynching. The photograph, which mimicked tropes of the hunt, featured the image of six black men dangling from a tree, accompanied by a single white man standing proudly, respectably dressed. hands draped behind his back. As the juxtaposition of image and text implied, lynching was the consequence of refusing chattel slavery following 1865.[34] Editors juxtaposed the photograph with an editorial on debt servitude that included the testimony of a white southerner named C. D. Rivers whose role as witness to a local lynching was used to corroborate *Crisis*'s claims of democratic declension. According to Rivers, lynching was a form of social control used to quell the potential of collective action in the "black belt," where black tenant farmers outnumbered white landowners. Rivers then narrated an incident in which a black community was decimated as a consequence of collective action against white violence.

The incident concerned a white overseer named Villipigue, who was killed after a group of black men retaliated on behalf of a boy with whom he'd been excessive. According to Rivers, Villipigue had

Figure 2.2. The Lynching in Lee County, Georgia. Crisis, January 20, 1916.

"thrashed" the boy "for some impudent reply" the boy had given him, which in turn stirred black residents, who sought recourse in an effort to deter future abuse. Rivers reasons that Villipigue would not have whipped the boy had he been white and that the purpose for his excessiveness was to induce the child's deference to and compliance with white authority.[35] The article provided no details as to how black residents engaged Villipigue other than to make clear that approaching him resulted in his death, white retaliation on the town, and the subsequent wounding and killing of black citizens. Rivers recalled how "Negroes for miles around" were terrorized. "Their secret society halls were burned, a church was burned . . . and several Negroes were shot." Targeting all blacks as well as institutions vital to black resistance sought to not simply terrorize but also murder the spirit of collective action against white supremacy. As Rivers explained, whites deemed such excessive violence "absolutely necessary to prevent the Negroes from taking revenge." Choosing to destroy foundational aspects of their community imparted upon them "that they should always be kept in mind of [the] swift and terrible penalties" that await them should they forget their place.[36]

Rivers's account of the retribution taken against this black community in response to the independent actions of a few illustrates that individual blacks did not simply endanger their own lives when they enacted a sense of agency contradictory to the one imagined for them but also the lives and livelihoods of all blacks when they dared believe themselves human. Because threat of sale, family separation, rape, and whipping were no longer available means of inducing compliance, explained Rivers, whites had to always be "ready to inflict capital punishment upon Negroes *violating that code which arises upon the relations of blacks and whites in the black belt.*"[37] Held in place by a specter of sadistic violence, this code of white racial order situated lynching as the ultimate response to expressions of black liberty. Like Wells's investigative reporting, *Crisis*'s coverage of the Lee County lynching provided readers an interpretive framework through which to read the images depicted in the photograph as emblems of a racist civic code. The report was succinct: five men were lynched for defending themselves against a system of exploitation that violated their constitutional rights. Such counterframing called the authenticity of the "black threat" narrative into question by guiding readers to interpret the drama captured in the Lee County photograph as a repeal of citizenship as opposed to a depiction of black savagery and white vulnerability. Such counterframing offered *Crisis*'s black readership a lesson in civics that figured white denial of the constitutional rights of blacks as a contradiction of democracy.

In instances where a photo was unavailable or considered a lapse of journalistic decorum, sketched reproductions of lynchings as produced by political cartoonists were used. For instance, preceding WWI, mainstream newspapers printed lengthy criticisms of overseas atrocities that conveyed compassion for the brutalities inflicted against foreigners; however, these critiques failed to address the brutalities inflicted upon citizens at home.[38] Black editorialists highlighting these omissions declared that America exposed the color of democracy when it rushed to denounce the barbaric, antidemocratic practices of other countries while such practices so clearly mirrored their own. Such critiques affirmed the falsity of America's projected ethos by raising the question of how the country could succeed in making the world safe for a global populace of liberty-loving citizens when it failed to secure the rights, liberties, and freedoms of its own people. As James Weldon Johnson rebuked, America was "a nation of hypocrites,"[39] and black newspapers reiterated this point time and time again when they drew parallels between America's attention to atrocities abroad and its indifference toward the atrocities enacted against citizens at home.[40]

The *Chicago Defender*'s 1916 "To the Presidential Nominee" is particularly noteworthy for the way it invoked the Lee County lynching photograph to forward this point. Three main features of the original image are echoed in the *Defender*'s political sketch: both images depict multiple victims, maintain the anonymity of the victims—neither *Crisis* nor the *Defender* identify victims by name— and appear in 1916, the year of the Lee County lynchings. Unlike in the photograph, however, the five men in the sketch are nude; the naked posterior of one occupies the foreground of the sketch, while silhouettes of the other four hang from branches in the back-

TO THE PRESIDENTIAL NOMINEE—

"No Citizen, Whatever Race, Color or Creed Is Safe Where Justice Sleeps and Anarchy Reigns and Where the Law Is Openly Defied."

"To the Presidential Nominee." "Shall the American Republic be pointed at with scorn by the foreign powers as a barbarous nation?," the *Chicago Defender* asked below this cartoon. "WE DEMAND PROTECTION from these murderers, even if the ENTIRE SOUTH MUST BE PLACED UNDER MARTIAL LAW. Why Mexico? Why bother about Germany or Japan? No civilized nation has disgraced itself with the above scenes in the past fifty years." From *Chicago Defender*, June 10, 1916.

Figure 2.3. "To the Presidential Nominee." Chicago Defender, June 10, 1916.

ground. Also worth noting is that although the photograph offers the semblance of victims' faces, the editorial reproduction offers none. Also distinguishing the photograph from the political sketch are the ways the image and memory of the five unidentified men are used. While *Crisis* uses the image to contend that lynching is an instrument of socioeconomic exploitation, the *Defender* uses the image to more directly assert the hypocrisy of American democracy. The paper accomplishes this in part through a rhetoric of shame established through its juxtaposition of image and text. The header and footer framing the image call the integrity of the presidential nominee into question while at the same time directing the public to consider how the international community would respond if it discovered America to be as treacherous as the countries it criticized. "Shall the American Republic be pointed at with scorn by the foreign powers as a barbarous nation?" asked the *Defender*. The paper emphasized American hypocrisy even further by calling into question how America could be so concerned with protecting the rights of foreigners and indicting foreign countries for their savagery while enacting the same injustices against citizens at home. "Why Mexico? Why bother about Germany or Japan? No civilized nation has disgraced itself with the above scenes in the past fifty years."[41] Such questions turned the lynching narrative on its head by shifting the conversation from one of white moral superiority to one of white depravity endorsed by the state. Within this context, the lynched black body was constructed as a symbol of democratic declension as it evidenced America's refusal to grant blacks the same constitutional rights and protections as whites. As the *Defender* implied, America was a morally depraved nation focused more on expanding its territory and safeguarding the rights of those abroad than safeguarding the rights of citizens at home.

Shaming the nation also included the use of lyching photographs that challenged standard images of the wonton brute. Lynching photographs often depicted a combination of partially clothed, charred, and dismembered corpses, at times draped with sheets that covered removed genitalia. Such images circulated among white supremacist enclaves galvanized support for lynching through visual tropes of the uncivil and depraved black beast. *Crisis*'s use of the James Clark lynching photograph is particularly interesting for the way it systematically contradicts such imaginings through a postmortem performance of respectability. The thirty-eight-year-old husband and father of three was a resident of Eau Gallie, Florida and a foundry worker who at the time of his death had been working as a personal driver for a salesman rooming at a local Eau Gallie hotel.[42] On July 13, 1926, the *Cocoa Tribune* reported news of Clark's July 11 lynching.

> It is said that the negro had been arrested Sunday for an attempted attack on a white girl of Eau Gallie, and that he was on his way, about 7:00 o'clock that evening, with the chief of police to Titusville for safe keeping, when the officer was over-powered by masked men. . . . [Clark] was whisked away, the body being found the next morning.[43]

Unlike many lynching victims, the body of James Clark was neither burned nor disfigured. His hands and feet remained intact, his body was fully clothed, and his neatly aligned slacks, kept up by the black belt around his waist, suggested that the appendage most coveted by lynchers was still intact. The only sign of restraint was the material used to bind his wrists. Aside from the rope about his neck, he is a bastion of respectability.

Crisis's recirculation of the photograph from February 1935 to January 1936 deviates from conventional use of such images in several ways. Typically, anti-lynching photographs were contextualized by information about the victim (when available) and the lynching event in a way that instructed readers on how to interpret images of black degradation as signs of "antidemocratic barbarism."[44] Detailing the names of lynching victims and their stories was a humanizing tactic that relocated the black body firmly within the civic imaginary. However, James Clark's identity remains undisclosed in this iteration of the photograph. Instead of a name, *Crisis* uses the article's headline, which reads "My Country, 'Tis of Thee, Sweet Land of Liberty—,"

My Country, 'Tis of Thee Sweet Land of Liberty—

This is a picture of what happens in America—*and no other place on earth!* Here is the U. S. rope and faggot record to date:

Lynchings since January 1:

1

●

Lynchings during same period last year:

0

●

Total lynchings since 1882:

5,069

●

(Figures as of January 15)

You can help stamp out lynch law by joining the forces who are campaigning for the passage of a federal anti-lynching law by the 74th congress. Write the N.A.A. C.P. for information: 69 Fifth Avenue, New York, N. Y.

Figure 2.4. "My Country, 'Tis of Thee, Sweet Land of Liberty—" The lynching of James Clark in Eau Gallie, Florida. Crisis, 1926.

to name Clark. The grammar of the image with particularity to the long dash situates Clark's lynched body as a manifestation of liberty in ways that invited readers to infer the relationship between liberty, respectability, and blackness: If the body of the respectably dressed lynching victim symbolized black liberty, then what, inferred *Crisis*, did the repression of black freedom look like?

Crisis's selection of a nameless and respectably dressed lynching victim eroded discursive constructions of blacks as subhuman beasts through a postmortem performance of middle-class respectability. Clark's white shirt, pressed slacks, tie, and belt depict a "neat" and orderly black citizen as opposed to a brutish enemy of the state. Juxtaposing his sensibly dressed lynched body with the lyrics of a patriotic hymn helped to solidify this claim by signifying on what *Crisis* inferred was a contradiction between the egalitarian ideals that frame American democracy and the deep rules of race and place that constituted its actual practice. Clark's facelessness, the fact that only his neck and portions of his chin and left cheek can be seen, amplifies the epideictic power in removing his name from the article. Rendering Clark faceless and nameless enhances the potential for identification between *Crisis*'s black readership and Clark's abject visage. Clark's constructed anonymity, which allowed *Crisis* readers to impart their own imaginings of who was the faceless, modestly dressed man dangling from the tree, drives home the message that the man without a full face and name could be, in fact, the reader's brother, father, son, nephew, uncle, or neighbor—perhaps even the reader. Through *Crisis*'s rhetorical recirculation of the image, Clark's lynched body and its eerie foreshadowing of what it means to be a member of the always already dead, came to index the precariousness of black citizenship during America's Great Depression.

The anti-lynching photograph "My Country, 'Tis of Thee," which *Crisis* ran for approximately two years, was a call to action. Although *Crisis*'s use of the James Clark image did not identify a victim or outline his story, its recontextualization and recirculation of the image as an index of antidemocratic barbarism rested squarely within

America's anti-lynching tradition. The caption, which read "This is a picture of what happens in America—and no other place on earth!" indicts America and challenges a national mythos that purports liberty, equality, and justice for all yet fails to safeguard these rights for black citizens. In this regard the photograph progresses from an invitation to identify with what white ways mean for black lives to a call for action that places everyday blacks like Clark at the helm of safeguarding their lives and the lives of those who look like them. This call is also an appeal to community, as it invites subscribers to "help stamp out lynch law by joining the forces who are campaigning for the passage of a federal anti-lynching law."[45] In the absence of a name, then, Clark's identity becomes fixed to a call for freedom that frames the passage of federal anti-lynching legislation as a key step to bringing the country closer in line with its governing principles.

Constructing White Innocence

Using the image of the black lynching victim to communicate the deep rules of democratic citizenship continued into the 1950s with the image of Emmett Louis Till. Emmett's lynching came just a year after the 1954 landmark decision of *Brown v. Board of Education*, which struck at the heart of white supremacy by invalidating the logic of "separate but equal" doctrine. Whites critical of the ruling organized. The Citizens' Council, which was referred to by some as the "up-town Klan,"[46] was a vocal grassroots collective whose adamant opposition to *Brown* turned on nineteenth-century claims of racial degradation via tropes of the black beast rapist, the innocent white maiden, and the chivalrous white hero. The Council contented that racial segregation was necessary because white women needed a defense against the licentiousness of black men and America needed a defense against mongrelization.[47] Such rhetoric metonymically constructing the white female body as a stand-in for America reasoned that to defend white womanhood against the threat of black penetration was to protect the nation against racial degradation. Desegregation transgressed the "ethical sanctions and standards" of democracy, argued Judge Brady, a leading member of the Citizens' Council. Foreshadowing Emmett's death, Brady asserted that such progressive moves were tantamount to a declaration of war; they were "invariably" constitutional attacks that would lead to "strife, bloodshed, and revolution."[48] As these citizens argued, segregation was a constitutional right that ensured the prosperity of the nation through its protection of a metonymical stand-in for the nation—that is, white women. Emmett's lynching, as it were, materialized this reality.

On August 20, 1955, Emmett Louis Till left Chicago, Illinois, for Money, Mississippi, to visit his great-uncle Moses Wright and cousins for the summer. On August 24 Emmett and his cousins went to Bryant's Grocery and Meat Market for candy. Emmett went inside to make a purchase and upon leaving reportedly whistled at and groped the store clerk, a twenty-one-year-old white woman named Carolyn Bryant, before leaving.[49] On August 27 Roy, Carolyn Bryant's husband, and his half-brother, J. W. Milam, kidnapped Emmett at gunpoint from his great-uncle's home around 2 a.m. When officials later followed up with Bryant and Milam, the two admitted to having kidnapped Emmett but denied having anything to do with his disappearance. On August 31 Emmett's body was discovered floating in the Tallahatchie River. The teen family lovingly called "Bobo" had been stripped naked, shot in the head, and tossed into the river with a seventy-five-pound gin fan tied to his neck.

Rather than release Emmett's body to his mother, Mamie Till-Mobley, Sumner County officials sought to hasten its burial without her knowledge or her permission.[50] Chicago mortician A. A. Rayner, who interceded on Mamie's behalf, successfully negotiated the release and transport of Emmett's remains, but only after agreeing to Sheriff C. H. Strider's terms that the casket remain sealed. On September 2, 1955, Mamie, her family, and various representatives of the press met Emmett's body at Chicago's Central Street Station.

Despite Strider's request that the casket remain closed, Mamie demanded that it be opened so that she could view the body and determine for herself if the remains belonged to the son she had sent to Mississippi. After verifying that the body was indeed Emmett's, Mamie insisted that the funeral be open casket. She would explain in later years that her purpose was to make "the whole nation bear witness"[51] to "what hatred of a human being, just because of color of skin, can do."[52] Her decision to flout Strider's directions by not just opening the casket but publicly displaying Emmett's body boldly defied the expected norm of black acquiescence to white authority in service of both inculcating viewers to racist hatred and cultivating a critical response to white supremacy. Demanding that America witness her son's death turned on the assertion that Emmett's life was a life that mattered—a life that deserved justice. As Courtney Baker explains, "it is the visibility of not only death itself but also the cause of death that compounds the affective," and to which I would add, the epideictic "power of the visual display."[53] Mamie's decision to "let them see what they did to [her] boy" transformed Emmett's lynched body into an epideictic text that communicated the extent whites would go to protect their imagined superiority. Following suit with her professed desire to teach "children all they need to know as they grow to become adults," Mamie's epidictic performance sought to inform the estimated 40,000 to 100,000[54] men, women, and children who walked through Chicago's Roberts Temple Church of Christ and, the thousands reading black news organs, of the precariousness of black life.

Milam and Bryant's defense turned on the constructed unrecognizability of Emmett's face. The trial consisted of five days of testimony and an all-white, all-male jury that deliberated for less than an hour before unanimously voting to acquit Roy Bryant and J. W. Milam of murder. During trial, Sheriff Strider, the official respondent on the case, conveniently avoided confirming Emmett's identity by avoiding to confirm the race of the remains. Strider testified that prolonged exposure to the water not only ruined the face of the remains but also rendered the body racially indistinguishable.[55] He explained that his only certainty with regard to the body examined on August 31 was that "it was a human being" and that it was "at least ten, if not fifteen" days in the river.[56] As to what kind of human—white full human or a black subhuman—the sheriff could not be certain. Dr. Luther B. Otken, the local physician called in by Strider to examine the body, testified that the corpse was so decomposed that neither a trained doctor nor a mother or a relative could have possibly been able to make a positive identification, given how mangled his face was.[57] Note how Otken's testimony functions both as testimony for the prosecution and as a tactical measure intended to discredit claims that the presumably unidentifiable body was Emmett's. Also worth noting is how both Strider and Otken rhetorically constructed white innocence by outright denying the truth.

Testimony for the state, which included the very people Otken claimed incapable of identifying the body, challenged the defense's narrative of unrecognizability. Emmett's great-uncle Moses Wright testified that he knew the remains pulled from the river were those of his great-nephew by the signet ring found on what remained of Emmett's right hand. He also positively identified Milam and Bryant as the two men who had come for Emmett the morning of August 27. Mamie's testimony confirmed Moses's, explained whom the ring originally belonged to, and how the reportedly unidentifiable body in the river came to have it. She said the silver ring engraved with the initials "L.T." and the date "May 25, 1943" found on the body had originally belonged to Louis Till, Emmett's late father,[58] and that she had gifted the ring to Emmett on the eve of his departure to Money. Despite this testimony, the jury rejected, along with the physical evidence, Moses's and Mamie's testimony, and timeline placing Milam and Bryant as the last to see Emmett because as one juror remarked, the brothers' guilt was never in question.[59]

While Sheriff Strider saw Emmett enough to certify through his signature that the body shipped to Chicago was indeed his, Strider's erasure of the boy during testimony reenacted the very civic disavowal performed during his lynching. This particular way of not seeing Emmett's black body invariably correlated to a particular way of misreading Emmett's black body as a body having no rights that the all-white, all-male jury must respect. Standing in for Emmett, then, was an indeterminate visage that within the context of American civic culture signified an unrecognizable, distorted humanity.

In January of the following year, and under protection from double jeopardy, Milam and Bryant confessed to both kidnapping and lynching Emmett in an exposé published in *Look* magazine. "The Shocking Story of Approved Killing in Mississippi" seemed fitting for a readership called to witness the second iteration of an American lynching. The interview detailed Milam and Bryant's encounter with Emmett from the point of his abduction to the point at which the brothers disposed of his body. Milam, who was particularly vocal, described Emmett as "hopeless." According to him, Emmett was a Negro who didn't recognize "his place" and had to be taught it.

> Well, what else could we do? . . . I'm no bully . . . I never hurt a nigger in my life, but as long as I live and can do anything about it, *niggers are gonna stay in their place. Niggers ain't gonna vote where I live. If they did, they'd control the government. They ain't gonna go to school with my kids. And when a nigger gets close to mentioning sex with a white woman, he's tired o' livin'. I'm likely to kill him. Me and my folks fought for this country, and we got some rights.* I stood there in that shed and listened to that nigger throw that poison at me, and I just made up my mind. 'Chicago boy,' I said, 'I'm tired of 'em sending your kind down here to stir up trouble. Goddam you, I'm going to make an example of you—just so everybody can know how me and my folks stand.[60]

The rationale forwarded here is a justification for lynching and at the same time a pledge to a white racial state that figures the disposal of "niggers [not in] their place" as national service. Milam's appeal figures Emmett's lynching as a symbolic means of reinstating the color line and as an emblem of his civic right to do so. According to him, Emmett was defiant, insolent, out of place and out of line because he allegedly refused to perform the deference Milam had come to expect. Additionally pressing for Milam was how Emmett allegedly spat "poison" by alluding to having had sex with a white woman. Given that white women figure as symbolic embodiments of the nation, Milam's contention that Emmett was "tired o' livin'" because of his admission and additional acts of insolence rhetorically framed the teen as a morally depraved menace that deserved the brutality he received. Casting Emmett as a social hazard displaced accountability to situate the fourteen-year-old as the cause of his own demise, rather than the two grown men who lynched him. Such rhetoric scapegoated Emmett via a racist logic that distinguished bullying from necessary acts of personal and national defense. As Milam reasoned, keeping "niggers . . . in their place" was not bullying, but rather a civil and judicious means of inducing compliance with the expected norms of white democracy. Like the black "Jacobins" of the past, Emmett willfully disregarded these norms and in doing so willfully forfeited his life. Following such reasoning, Emmett was either insane on account of willfully refusing to observe his place or because he wanted to die. Either way transforming him into a paradigmatic example of the consequences of desegregation was a rhetorical performance that sought to teach all Negroes, despite progressive legislation, that America would remain a land of white racial rule.

A Lesson in Civics

For blacks, Mamie Till-Mobley's decision to let the world "see what they did to my boy" transformed Emmett's supposedly unrecognizable visage into a symbol that indexed the precariousness of black citizenship. *Jet* magazine, which was one of the most widely circulated among America's black citizenry, was a chief vehicle for Mamie's message. *Jet's* coverage of the trial inculcated black readers to the color of American democracy as Emmett's photos communicated the judicial system's investment in sustaining the civic supremacy of whiteness. Coverage consisted of a photo-essay that included a holiday photo of a respectably dressed Emmett and the postmortem photograph of his respectably dressed corpse. Like the 1916 lynching photograph of James Clark, the 1955 image of a tastefully dressed Emmett invoked a middle-class respectability that framed Emmett as the "good" Negro boy.

Jet's coverage of the incident participated in a long tradition of educating blacks in white ways. As Trudier Harris reminds, deploying narratives and tropes of lynching as definitive guides for navigating a racist democracy was a rhetorically constitutive act of community that communicated "white attitudes towards Blacks" in ways that urged black readers to "identify with what those attitudes have meant in terms of destruction" for them.[61] Such work contributed to the repository of black experiential knowledge used to combat the silencing and historical forgetting of not just lynching, but also lynching's relationship to the state. This "critical black memory," as Leigh Raiford describes it, offered members of the black community a blueprint for surviving institutional racism that carried hope for a better tomorrow at the same time it carried disappointment over past failures to produce transformative change.[62] Mamie's decision to publicize Emmett's lynching eulogized him in ways that encouraged black readers to verify their place within the political spectrum through their public role as witnesses to his murder.[63] Emmett's lynching and the postmortem photos that followed imparted crucial knowledge to black readers regarding their place within America's political imaginary. The lesson Student Non-Violent Coordinating Committee (SNCC) leader Cleveland Sellers gained after seeing the *Jet* photograph was that his right to life and liberty did not equate to a white right to murder blacks with impunity. Sellers, who was just twelve at the time, explained his ability to identify with Emmett despite what he could only describe as "a ragged, rotting sponge" of a face:

I tried to put myself in his place and imagine what he was thinking when those white men took him from his home that night.
I wondered how I could have handled the situation. I read and
reread the newspapers and magazine accounts. I couldn't get over
the fact that the men who were accused of killing him had not
been punished at all.[64]

Fellow SNCC organizer and civil rights activist Anne Moody was
fourteen the year Emmett was murdered. Moody, who had first
heard news of Emmett's lynching from schoolmates, was firmly
warned to play dumb when she asked her mother about the incident.

"Mama, did you hear about that fourteen-year-old Negro boy who
was killed a little over a week ago by some white men?" I asked her.
"Where did you hear that?" she said angrily.
" . . . I heard Eddie them talking about it this evening coming from
school."
"Eddie them better watch how they go around here talking. These
white folks git a hold of it they gonna be in trouble," she said.
"What are they gonna be in trouble about, Mama? People got a
right to talk, ain't they?"
"You go on to work before you is late. And don't you let on like
you know nothing about that boy being killed before Miss Burke and
them. Just do your work like you don't know nothing." she said. "That
boy's a lot better off in heaven than he is here."[65]

Moody, however, was unable to avoid discussing the incident because
of Mrs. Burke's desire to make a point. When she asked Moody if
she had heard of the boy killed in Mississippi, Moody, recalling her
mother's instructions, lied and replied, "No." Mrs. Burke pressed on,
"Do you know why he was killed?" Moody remained silent. "He was
killed because he got out of his place with a white woman," Mrs.
Burke continued. What followed, Moody explained, was a diatribe

about sassy Negroes having "no respect," threaded with warnings from Mrs. Burke to Moody about the dangers of forgetting her place. Like Milam, Mrs. Burke wielded Emmett's lynching as a cautionary tale on insolence, and this is what impacted Moody the most. Recalling the incident in her memoir, Moody wrote, "I went home shaking like a leaf on a tree. For the first time out of all her trying, Mrs. Burke had made me feel like rotten garbage. Many times she had tried to instill fear within me and subdue me. . . . But when she talked about Emmett Till there was something in her voice that sent chills and fear all over me."

The magnitude of the exchange sank in as Moody recalled Mrs. Burke's validation alongside her own mother's instruction to mask her knowledge of the murder. Whereas Moody originally questioned her mother's instructions to feign ignorance, she later came to recognize their importance. Being exposed to the hypocrisy of American democracy exposed the fourteen-year-old Moody to "a new fear," specifically, "the fear of being killed just because I was black."[66]

For Myrlie Evers-Williams, the wife of the late NAACP Mississippi field director Medgar Evers, Emmett's image depicted "the story in microcosm of every Negro in Mississippi," for his lynching and the freedom of his murderers demonstrated that white supremacy would continue to remain anchored in the destruction of black bodies and that white Americans throughout the state "would uphold such killings through their police and newspapers and courts of law." As Evers-Williams understood, Emmett's lynching and the photographic evidence to support it "was the proof . . . that no Negro's life was really safe, and that the federal government was either powerless, as it claimed, or simply unwilling to step in."[67]

Writer John Edgar Wideman reiterated this point in his 1998 essay "Looking at Emmett Till." The essay, which was written while reflecting on the June 1998 lynching of James Byrd, narrated the trauma around Wideman's initial experience with the image of Emmett Till. Like so many others, Wideman learned about Emmett through *Jet*'s coverage of his murder trial. "I *certainly hadn't* been searching for Emmett Till's picture in *Jet*. It found me. A blurred, grayish something resembling an aerial snapshot of a landscape cratered by bombs or ravaged by natural disaster." By the time Wideman realized that "the thing in the photo was a dead black boy's face" and jerked his eyes away, it was too late.[68] The impact of Wideman's struggle not to look despite having done so and the trauma it engenders manifests as a "nightmare of being chased" by a monstrous face "too terrifying for the dream to reveal."[69] His struggle to not look is in part a consequence of his tortured identification with Emmett. Identifying with Emmett means that Wideman must acknowledge what the image of Emmett's "crushed, chewed, mutilated, and gray and swollen" face signifies for him,[70] and to do that means that Wideman must acknowledge how his own mutilated body figures as a symbol of democratic declension. As he explained, in addition to being fourteen the year Emmett was lynched, Wideman, like Emmett, was also on his way to high school, boisterous and proud, and prone to peer pressure.[71] The ubiquity of these qualities, namely, that they could belong to any black boy, drives Wideman's terror as they mark him as a member of the always already soon-to-be-dead. Speaking to the disposability of black Americans,

> Sometimes I think the only way to end this would be with Andy Warhol-like strips of images, the same face, Emmett Till's face, replicated twelve, twenty-four, forty-eight, ninety-six times on a wall-sized canvas . . . each version of the face exactly like the other but different names printed below each one. Martin Luther Till. Malcolm Till. Medgar Till. Nat Till. Gabriel Till. Michael Till. Huey Till. Bigger Till. Nelson Till. Mumia Till. Colin Till. Jesse Till. Your daddy, your mama, your sister, brother, aunty, cousin, uncle, niece, nephew Till.[72]

Wideman's artistic configuration of Till as reiterated in this Warhol-like imagining rhetorically figured the fourteen-year-old boy as a pattern of experience particular to black men but applicable to blacks in general. For Wideman, Emmett's photograph indexed an "apartheid mentality" rooted in America's original sin of slavery and a white prerogative in place since Milam's and Bryant's "ancestors imported Emmett Till's ancestors to these shores."[73] Emmett's abject body, then, is emblematic of a "determined unwillingness," Wideman explained, to surrender the advantages of white racial privilege.[74] As he explained, the moral psychology of whites framed denying the humanity of others as "more acceptable . . . than placing themselves, their inherited dominance, at risk"; consequently, "Emmett Till dies again and again because his murder, the conditions that ensure and perpetuate it, have not been honestly examined."[75] It is this unwillingness that made the forty-nine-year-old James Byrd the next node of a tradition. On June 7, 1998, the Jasper, Texas, native accepted a ride from three white men, who severely beat him, chained his ankles to the back of their pickup truck, and dragged him until he was decapitated.[76] If the image of Emmett Till symbolized an effort to "slay an entire generation" and push them "backward to the bad old days when our lives seemed not to belong" to them,[77] then Byrd's lynching, concluded Wideman, was a reaffirmation that this was "the way things have always been, will always be, the way they're supposed to be."[78] For Wideman, as with others, the image of Emmett Louis Till indexed America's ongoing investment in a white democracy.

Conclusion

The civic resonance of lynching photography resides in its dissemination of differing visions of democracy. As Baker observes, the "visibly dead body not only instructs the spectator on issues of mortality but also illustrates the sometimes frustrating relationship between morality and justice."[79] Lynching photographs functioned as visual topoi of white supremacy's tie to the legally codified script of white racial terrorism. As such, these photographs served as a repository of civic life in that they offered citizens across the color line a visual vocabulary for the "deep rules" of democracy. Whether used to promote or denounce, images of lynching modeled citizenship as a racialized order in which white liberty was defined as the right to kill blacks with impunity.

CHAPTER THREE
A PAST NOT YET PASSED

They have gone from strange fruit to just shoot.
—ATTENDEE, 2000 New-York Historical Society *Without Sanctuary*
exhibition

At the turn of the twenty-first century, museum and cultural center executives motivated by a desire to highlight the coexistence
of American racism and egalitarian principles circulated a collection of lynching photography called *Without Sanctuary: Lynching
Photographs in America*. Composed of over 100 lynching photographs, postcards, and artifacts, *Without Sanctuary* depicted men and
women, blacks, Jews, and Mexicans lynched, burned, and surrounded
by crowds of smiling white onlookers. The first installation of the collection was not called *Without Sanctuary*, but rather *Witness*, and was
displayed in Manhattan at the Roth Horowitz gallery's millennium
exhibition from January 13 to February 12, 2000.[1] The exhibition,
which consisted of approximately twenty lynching photographs and
postcards with minimal textual commentary and even less historical
contextualization, was acquired for the way it "reveal[ed] history" at
the turn of the century. In showcasing *Witness*, Andrew Roth sought
to give citizens a sense of where the nation had been, in an effort
to help it gather a sense of where it might be going.[2] His efforts to

cultivate a reflective national public situated the collection as both a flashback and conceivable foreshadowing of race relations in the twenty-first century.

In the previous chapter I examined how the epideictic rhetoric of lynching photographs inculcated citizens along the color line in racialized performances of American identity. Here I continue that exploration to consider how the epideictic rhetoric of *Without Sanctuary* offered contemporary citizens an interpretive lens for reading present-day iterations of state-sanctioned antiblack violence. As I outline here, the rhetoric of the installation cultivated public memory of lynching by drawing continuity between the nation's past and present proclivity for antiblack violence. In doing so, museums and cultural centers that hosted the collection helped to facilitate a critical democratic literacy that aided citizens in reading how lynching's supposedly long-ago past continues to reverberate in the present.

Without Sanctuary: A Lesson in Civics Continued

Central to this twenty-first-century recirculation of lynching photographs was the intent to use images of the past as a means of contextualizing the present. Artifacts placed within the context of a museum or a historical or cultural center do not present "lessons" or "arguments" on account of simply being housed within those spaces, but rather because of being pressed into meaning by the wall panels, wall text, brochures, audio, video, lighting, and overall architecture of those spaces. These features of what Schwartz calls the "exhibition apparatus" work to build a narrative context and a rationale for their display.[3] Requests for *Without Sanctuary* stemmed from the way the collection spoke to contemporary iterations of black death and state-sanctioned racialized terror. The police torture of Abner Louima (1997) and the killings of Amadou Diallo (1999) and Patrick Dorismond (2000) at the hands of city police were three incidents

among a litany that contextualized the collection's year-long installation in New York. On August 9, 1997, after being accused of punch-
ing an officer in a scuffle, thirty-year-old Haitian immigrant Abner
Louima was beaten while being transported to the 70th Precinct,
strip-searched, and later sodomized by officers with a broom han-
dle.[4] On February 4, 1999, twenty-three-year-old Amadou Diallo
was riddled with forty-one bullets when four plainclothes officers
opened fire as he stood in the vestibule of his apartment. Diallo,
who had been misidentified by officers as a serial rapist long since
in police custody, had been reaching for identification as directed
when he was shot.[5] In the weeks that followed, New York City mayor
Rudy Giuliani defended the four officers through statements that
equated the violation of Diallo's rights and the taking of Diallo's life
with the officers' own fear of persecution. "The death of Amadou
Diallo was a great tragedy," began Giuliani. "We express once again
our sympathy. . . . There is no way we can comprehend what it means
to lose a child." However, he also said we must recognize that the
officers involved "have also gone through a nightmare."[6] Here,
Giuliani's apologist stance likens killing to indignity, and death to
shame, in an effort to court sympathy for the officers. Equating the
killing of an innocent, unarmed man to the humiliation of being
(rightly) accused of murder as an officer of the law gravely reduced
the value of Diallo's black life by reasoning that the public should be
as passionate about proving the officers' innocence as they should
be about seeking redress for the loss of Diallo's life. As Giuliani reasoned, the "nightmare" of being perceived as a murderer (as opposed
to a threat) likewise demanded the community's compassion.

Several months later, on March 16, 2000, twenty-six-year-old
Patrick Dorismond was shot and killed after being propositioned
for drugs by an undercover officer outside a local nightclub.[7] The
officer and Dorismond, who was reportedly irritated over being
approached, exchanged words. A fight ensued, at which point
Dorismond was shot by another undercover officer, Det. Anthony
Vasquez, who feared for the safety of his partner. Giuliani's defense

of Vasquez was particularly demonizing. In the days following the
event, Giuliani authorized the release of Dorismond's arrest record
under the guise that it revealed a "'pattern of behavior'" that made
Dorismond—not the officer—accountable for his death. As he
argued through the report, Dorismond was "no altar boy" but in fact
someone whose past actions "may justify . . . what the police officer
did."[8] Giuliani's rhetoric perpetuated racist imaginings of the black
threat as a means of directing attention away from officers'culpability
to that of the assumed guilt of the victim. Depicting Dorismond as
the opposite of godly vilified him before the public to the benefit of
the officers that killed him and the state apparatus that sanctioned
his killing. Such scapegoating recast Dorismond as someone worthy
of the brutality he received, as opposed to an innocent man whose
rights were violated on account of being racially profiled.

In each case the state seemed to agree with Giuliani's assess-
ments of black guilt and blue innocence. In the torture of Abner
Louima, only two of the five officers involved received sentences,[9]
all four officers involved in Amado Diallo's death were acquitted,
and in the case of Dorismond, the officer who shot and killed him
was never indicted. *Without Sanctuary*'s potential to contextualize
community unrest over these and other incidents of unmitigated
police brutality throughout the tristate area is what motivated the
New-York Historical Society director Steward Desmond's visit to
the Roth and his later acquisition of the collection. As he explained,
the N-YHS's desire to show *Without Sanctuary* stemmed from a
consideration of "how a historical perspective [on race relations in
America] might inform this controversy and allow an interracial
dialogue that reached beyond [criticism]" and finger pointing.[10]
Lynching is "something we should know about and remember,"
echoed N-YHS President, Betsy Gotbaum, "especially in the context of black distrust of the New York City police."[11] The N-YHS's
installation, which showcased the collection from March 2000 to
October of that year, was the first official installation of *Without
Sanctuary* under its original name. Unlike the Roth, the N-YHS's

installation matted, framed, labeled, and displayed the photographs with explanatory wall panels and text, and further contextualized the collection with pamphlets and broadsides from the anti-lynching movement, information on leading African Americans in politics and the arts, and spaces where attendees were encouraged to process their experience with *Without Sanctuary* through written comment and educator-facilitated dialogue.[12]

The prevailing narrative that contextualized this and later installations explained how lynching served white supremacy and imaginings of a white racial state. The N-YHS demonstrated this in the way it centralized the critiques of figures such as Ida B. Wells, Frederick Douglass, and Walter White; outlined the collective push for anti-lynching legislation by organizations like the NAACP, the Commission on Interracial Communication (CIC), and the Association of Southern Women for the Prevention of Lynching (ASWPL); and figured the nation's failure to pass anti-lynching legislation as evidence of its refusal to recognize the constitutional rights of black citizens. At the Warhol Museum in Pittsburgh, the city's history of racism, racist violence, anti-lynching activism, and the racially motivated mass killing of six residents by a white man in April 2000[13] provided exigent moments for *Without Sanctuary*'s installation. The exhibition included a map of lynchings throughout the country, a pastiche mural of local and national hate crimes created by a local Pittsburgh artist, and a forty-foot illustrated timeline from 1895 to 1995, both of which depicted hate crimes as part of America's lynching tradition.[14] The Warhol installation also included an expanded history of the black-owned and black-operated newspaper the *Pittsburgh Courier*, which was known to be so vocal in its opposition to lynching that southern communities often banned its distribution or burned it.[15] Exhibiting the history of the *Courier* in conjunction with the collection localized lynching and the anti-lynching movement for attendees while chronicling the contributions of Pittsburgh's black community to the struggle for racial justice. Additional features of the Pittsburgh installation included interactive stations, such as the listening station where current attendees listened and watched video-recorded reflections of *Without Sanctuary* left by previous visitors, comment books in which visitors documented their experience with the collection for posterity, facilitator-directed discussion forums that encouraged reflection and dialogue among visitors, and the "Postcard to Tolerance" station in which visitors adapted the lynching postcard tradition to more ethical ends. Activities such as these that invited attendees to critically engage the past, in kind facilitated public memory of American lynching through a multimodal lesson about Pittsburgh's role in the anti-lynching movement, the city's own racist past, and contemporary iterations of racist violence against blacks.

Localizing the collection's message was chief to educating attendees on the pervasiveness of American lynching. Installations at both the Levine Museum of the New South in Charlotte, North Carolina, and the Charles H. Wright Museum in Detroit, Michigan, among other cities, utilized local histories of racist violence to draw continuity between the past and the present. One station at the Levine Museum installation called "It Happens Here: Carolina Lynchings," documented more than 260 lynchings between North and South Carolina.[16] Further localizing the exhibit was news of a Charlotte incident in which a resident displayed a lynched Obama effigy on his lawn.[17] Another section of the Levine exhibition, which included a voting station accompanied by a bulletin board with recent news articles regarding several killings labeled "lynchings," invited attendees to consider the relationship between lynching and contemporary violence against blacks. As Levine staff historian Tom Hanchett explained, the purpose of stations such as this one was to encourage attendees to "weigh in on" questions exploring the continuance of lynching culture today.[18] Similarly, at the Charles H. Wright Museum, interactive stations, comment panels, comment books, and interactive kiosks like those at the N-YHS, Warhol, and Levine, engaged attendees in a series of questions regarding *Without Sanctuary*'s relevance to a twenty-first-century public.

"They Have Gone from Strange Fruit to Just Shoot"

In addition to interactive stations and face-to-face and online discussion forums, installations of *Without Sanctuary* also utilized soundscapes and lighting to direct attendee responses. The Levine Museum installation in Charlotte, Atlanta's installation at the King Center, and the collection's later installation at Cincinnati's Underground Railroad Freedom Center blended renditions of Negro spirituals, Billie Holiday's anti-lynching anthem "Strange Fruit," dark lighting, and the sound of chirping crickets to induce a sense of discomfort and unrest among visitors. This "menacing" soundtrack, as one King Center visitor described it, invoked a sense of impending doom that followed visitors as they progressed through the narrow corridor of the dimly lit anteroom and into the exhibition space proper.[19] The ambience established through the use of soundscapes, lighting, dark-colored walls, and dark carpeting enhanced *Without Sanctuary*'s character as a site of mourning and remembrance.

In the case of *Without Sanctuary*, exigent moments such as the unabated killing of black men combined with the exhibition apparatus, lynching photographs and artifacts from the anti-lynching movement to produce a narrative that used evidence of America's racist past to argue for a particular interpretation of its present. Visitors synthesized this information to draw particular conclusions about America's history of lynching. As one attendee remarked, "We enter 2000 not so differently than when [sic] entered 1900. The method of execution has changed but the hatred and racism behind it although hidden remain the same."[20] In other instances, attendees read antiblack policing by citizens in and out of white sheets as a precursor to the policing of blacks by citizens in and out of blue uniforms. Attendees synthesized historical facts from *Without Sanctuary* to read contemporary incidents such as the 1999 "shooting death" of Amadou Diallo as part of America's lynching tradition. As one attendee concluded, "They have gone from strange fruit to just shoot."[21] "Modern day lynch mobs don't use ropes now," remarked

Chris Easley. "[T]hey use guns" and a badge.[22] Ayesha Grice was detailed in her response,

> Four police officers were acquitted of any charges after shooting an unarmed man to death. The Mayor says the verdict was just, and that there was no reason to change police policies. In other words its [sic] alright to kill an unarmed man as long as he is Black. We also are faced with the fact that the death penalty is legal and that many innocent Black people have died in state sanctioned murders. I wish I could say that things are better now, but maybe what my daughter said was true. They've traded in their ropes for guns and a badge and a hypodermic needle. The fact remains the same. Innocent people of one race are still being murdered by the descendants of the people in your photographs. God have mercy on us all.[23]

Grice's read of Diallo's death as a modern-day lynching, which signifies on the correlation between the denial of due process under lynching and the denial of due process under antiblack policing, is neither anachronistic nor hyperbolic. Diallo's killing, as Grice points out, shares a number of similarities with lynchings of the late nineteenth and early twentieth century. To begin, Diallo was, within the context of US racial categorizations, "black"; he, like many lynching victims, was innocent of the crime he was accused of committing; he, like many lynching victims, was denied due process of law on account of being black, which invariably correlates to "guilty," and his killers, like lynchers, were legitimated by the state through language that rendered actions otherwise considered criminal, reasonable and just. Grice's lament, like those of others, draws a correlation between bodies in blue and white power to conclude that the racist ideology depicted in *Without Sanctuary* is the same racist ideology that informs and legitimates America's targeted eradication and incarceration of contemporary black citizens.

Memorializing Victims of Lynching

Lynchings were scenes of spectacle violence, scenes in which the disavowal of civic rights and the destruction of black life were boisterously celebrated as opposed to grieved. *Without Sanctuary* challenged this ritual performance of white citizenship in the way it memorialized victims of lynching. In Pittsburgh and Atlanta exhibitors transformed opening-day programs into funerary ceremonies composed of elegies, the recitation of scripture, and eulogies that condemned the injustice victims suffered, the struggle families and communities affected by racial terrorism experienced, and the generational trauma of lynching. At *Without Sanctuary*'s reveal in Pittsburgh, opening-day ceremonies consisted of interfaith prayer services as well as a choir concert with local resident Rev. Deryck Mitchell, who led the Warhol Choir in a rendition of "Amazing Grace."[24] Formally referred to as the "Day of Remembrance," Atlanta's opening-day ceremony, held at the historic Ebenezer Baptist Church and church-home of civil rights leader Martin Luther King Jr., welcomed the families of Georgia lynching victim Murray Burton and Georgia lynching survivor Winfred Rembert, who functioned as living, speaking testaments to the generational trauma of lynching.[25] The ritual pouring of libation to the ancestors and a benediction that named "the parties involved in lynching—the victims, their families and communities, the lynchers, their families, the bystanders, those who kept quiet, the photographers and postcard artists, printers, and mongers" was also given.[26] The act of naming is a chief feature of memory and restorative justice work. As a counter-rhetoric of lynching gained traction in the states, intermittent efforts to bring perpetrators to justice was hindered by a rhetoric of silence among whites that commonly attributed lynchings to "persons unknown."[27] Naming victims, perpetrators, those who acquiesced, and families of victims rescues lynching victims from the shroud of silence that compounded the injustice of their deaths and that contributed to their national forgetting while at the same time permitting contemporary citizens the opportunity to begin the preliminary work of transferring historical truths once considered portions of America's "unusable" past to the realm of its "usable" present.

The collection's installation at Cincinnati's Underground Railroad Freedom Center in 2010 and Charlotte's Levine Museum of the New South in 2012 also opened with ceremonies that included benedictions, narrations of a violent past and violent present, and explicit calls for a more critical understanding of the connection between lynching and present-day acts of racialized violence. Although not at an official memorial service, attendees of the Freedom Center's opening ceremony wore dark attire, spoke in hushed tones, and presented somber faces during opening remarks. As then-CEO and Freedom Center president Donald Murphy asserted, "In looking back, *Without Sanctuary: Lynching Photographs in America* reveals real victims who deserve acknowledgement and honor."[28] The opening ceremony, which took place in the Center's "Pavilion of Courage," introduced the collection, outlined the history of lynching, and placed *Without Sanctuary* within the larger context of Ohio's position as a free border state to the slave state of Kentucky. The Underground Railroad Freedom Center's southern-facing position on the Ohio River is representative of the system of hidden networks that transported enslaved blacks from the slave state of Kentucky into the free state of Ohio. The museum's Eternal Flame, which burns steadily from an upper-level floor overlooking the Ohio River and Kentucky shoreline, reenacts the practice of signaling safety and refuge to those escaping bondage. Underground Railroad operators placed candles in the windows of their homes or businesses to signal that such spaces were safe spaces. Many of those who were able to escape Kentucky followed these signs to eventually settle into the black quarters of Cincinnati. Such reenactments, in addition to the museum's geographical location, framed it as a beacon of hope, freedom, and sanctuary to those constitutionally denied America's promise.

Charlotte's Levine Museum of the New South operated similarly; however, it was the exhibition's conclusion, rather than its opening, that carried the trappings of a memorial service. "Without Sanctuary: A Conference on Lynching and the American South" was hosted by the University of North Carolina-Charlotte during October of 2012 in conjunction with the Levine's September 29–December 31 installation of *Without Sanctuary*. The conference concluded at the historic First Presbyterian Church in downtown Charlotte with an address from historian Claude Clegg. Conference attendees, local residents, and visitors of the Levine who had walked from the day's last showing of the collection at the museum to the church some ten minutes away, were greeted by First Presbyterian parishioners and members as they proceeded through the door. The ceremony opened with a benediction delivered by the church's pastor that included a call to remembrance and vigilance against racism and racist violence before the congregation sang a hymn. The night ended with an address from Clegg, who contextualized the history of lynching in North Carolina before reading a selection from his 2010 work *Troubled Ground*, which documents the history of the 1906 lynching of three black men in Salisbury, North Carolina.

Without Sanctuary was awash in ritual that transformed the body and life of lynching victims into "equipment for living."[29] Similar to how lynching and burning narratives and lynching plays and performances offered black audiences new ways of coping and navigating racial terrorism,[30] so too did ritual performances. Pouring libation; speaking the names of the deceased, their murderers, and co-conspirators; interfaith prayer services; and hymn singing illustrated just a few ways in which blacks, as Koritha Mitchell outlines, lived with lynching. These rituals alongside narratives of how lynching victims lived and died eulogized them in ways that permitted the injustice of their deaths to stand as paradigmatic examples[31] of what democracy has meant in terms of destruction for blacks. The eulogistic rhetoric of the installations, then, forwarded a powerful counter-rhetoric to the discourse that legitimated and celebrated lynching. This counter-

rhetoric humanized lynching victims not only as individuals deserving of justice but also as individuals deserving of remembrance. It
asserted that the lives of lynching victims were lives worth remembering, that the lives of lynching victims were lives that mattered,
and that America was far from achieving "the dream," as the injustice of these deaths lived on through continued assaults on black
life. The eulogistic rhetoric of these collections, specifically, their call
to remember victims of lynching alongside present-day victims of
antiblack violence and police brutality, drew continuity between the
past and present in ways that echoed the NAACP's understanding of
lynching as an adaptive, dynamic, and transformative performance.
Like the NAACP, *Without Sanctuary* demonstrates that lynching
isn't dead and gone, but still very much a part of the present.

Without Sanctuary's use of the past in service of the present is
chief to how memorial rhetorics inculcate citizens to particular values, attitudes, and ideals. They play a key role in the construction
and maintenance of community by projecting attributes and principles deemed worthy of reverence and adoption by the community.[32]
Memorials serve as a "species of pedagogy"[33] in that they condense
and fix "moral lessons of history" for posterity.[34] Unlike traditional
stone and stationary lynching memorials such as the Clayton Jackson
McGhie Memorial in Duluth, Minnesota, *Without Sanctuary* is a
nationally circulated, multimodal memorial site whose epideictic
rhetoric challenges the colorblind logic of the late twentieth century
through a rhetoric of memory that invites attendees to read continuity between America's violent and racist past and its equally violent
and racist present. As Erika Doss explains, "shame-based memorials" like those that address slavery and lynching draw attention to
questions of rights, representation, and citizenship in ways that challenge the grand narrative of equality, liberty, and progress espoused
in national discourse.[35] These memorials work differently in what
they compel citizens to remember and adopt and what they encourage citizens to feel. Like preceding circulations of anti-lynching pho-

tography that situated lynching as a break from America's ideals of freedom, liberty, and equality, *Without Sanctuary* encoded values of equality and humility onto lynching victims in ways that shifted the signification of the victim from abject object worthy of scorn to citizen-neighbor worthy of compassion and justice. For contemporary victims of lynching remembered at these installations, such work humanizes them in the wake of discourse that scapegoats and demonizes them.

This is not to say that *Without Sanctuary* is not without its complications. The ethical complexities of looking and witnessing as they apply to the collection have been the center of critical debate. In "Without Sanctuary: Bearing Witness: Bearing Whiteness," Wendy Wolters declares that *Without Sanctuary* fails as a memorial site because it reproduces, "rather than interrupts, the power relations of (black) lynching victim and (white) lynching spectator."[36] Her critique of looking at images of lynching asserts that the empathy constructing contemporary looking prevents identification with victims. Accordingly, *Without Sanctuary* fails as a memorial site because, rather than behold black suffering, the impulse to empathize and identify with the victim—that is, to place the self in the position of the racialized "other"—prevents the viewer from truly "witnessing" the full horror of lynching, as looking at lynching photographs invites and simultaneously precludes identification. As Wolters explains,

> Our "good intentions" in looking, our intent to identify with the black suffering body, "increases the difficulty of beholding black suffering since the endeavor to bring pain close exploits the spectacle of the body in pain and oddly confirms the spectral character of suffering and the inability to witness the captive's pain."[37]

In sum, Wolters contends that *Without Sanctuary's* attempt to create witnesses through the practice of looking at black victimization inadvertently reproduces the original scene of the lynching spectacle as well as the white gaze that accompanies it.[38] Historian Grace Elizabeth Hale echoes Wolter's point, asserting that *Without Sanctuary* "foreground[ed] violence as a defining characteristic of whiteness" and "victimization as the defining characteristic of blackness."[39] In a review of the collection's New York exhibition and the coffee table book that later followed, Michael Eric Dyson exclaimed similarly, "To commercialize the suffering of black people is to do the ultimate disservice to black people."[40] Contending there was little, if any, difference between contemporary viewers and viewing publics of the past, critics like Wolters, Hale, and Dyson maintained that rather than evoke critical reflection, *Without Sanctuary* instead did nothing more than produce contemporary voyeurs of black victimization.[41]

To be clear, the sentiment expressed by these critics is shared. To dismiss the complications of looking with regard to the recirculation of lynching photographs would be critically irresponsible. However, excluded from much of this criticism is a consideration of the exigencies that brought *Without Sanctuary* into being. Depiction of the grotesque is without doubt always conflicted; it is never innocent and it is never clean but rather always fraught with complications.[42] What I'd like to highlight here, however, is how this twenty-first-century circulation participates in a tradition of reflecting white attitudes toward blacks as a blueprint for civic life. The exigent moments occasioning *Without Sanctuary*'s arrival—that is, community outrage over the state-sanctioned killing of innocent blacks by police—in conjunction with the narrative of historical injustice, national complicity, and black activism forwarded by the exhibition apparatus are significant factors that contributed to the collection's reception. While situating the collection within both local and national discourses of civil and human rights may not altogether shatter the white gaze, attendees' response to *Without Sanctuary* demonstrated that such framing can, in significant ways, contribute to its disruption. In this sense, we cannot discount how context affects reception, nor can we discount how this twenty-first-century recirculation participates in a larger rhetorical culture in which images of black victimization are used to communicate vital lessons about civic belonging in America.

Conclusion

In 2005, on the fiftieth anniversary of Emmett Till's murder, the Senate issued a national apology for its failure to enact anti-lynching legislation. Motivation for the apology came as a direct result of senators' experience with the coffee table book *Without Sanctuary*. They had been moved to recognize the nation's accountability and to acknowledge, as Virginia Republican senator George Allen explained, "The Senate had failed these Americans." "If we truly want to move forward," he continued, "we must admit that failure and learn from it."[43]

America's history of lynching is a narrative of political rupture that illustrates the hypocrisy of American democracy. At *Without Sanctuary*, citizens learned of America's persecution of black members of the polity, of America's surveillance and policing of black life, and of the precariousness of being a second-class citizen. As Randall Burkett remarked, *Without Sanctuary* illustrated that racist violence was not uncommon to America, but rather an endemic American folkway. "These images document the reality and depth of racism that have been a central dynamic in American history." They illustrate that "[w]e are not unlike the rest of the world in our ability to perpetuate violence, though we imagine ourselves exempt from this evil."[44]

While bearing witness denies that there is a "best way of depicting or thinking about atrocities," it does imply that "the very fact of paying heed collectively is crucial."[45] As one attendee concluded, "Lynching was a statement trumpeting the ultimate power of white men and a crude form of advertising, alerting black citizens that, in the wake of emancipation, they would do well to 'know their place' and act accordingly."[46] Installations of *Without Sanctuary* exemplified how supposed deviations from the national script were part of a larger ideological framework that undermined democracy in its devaluation of black life. Inviting attendees to bear witness to the comfortable coexistence of egalitarian ideals and state-sanctioned violence against blacks directed them to consider how the myth of American exceptionalism has been and continues to be shaped by an ardent disavowal of democratic principles.

CHAPTER FOUR

LYNCHING IN THE AGE OF OBAMA

*White folks, whatever their talk of freedom and liberty, would
not allow a black president. . . . A black president signing a bill
into law might as well sign his own death certificate.*
—Ta-Nehisi Coates, "Fear of a Black President"[1]

In previous chapters I traced how the us/them dialectic informing
the ideological and rhetorical construction of "the people" likewise
informed lynching's civic resonance, how lynching functioned as a
violent rhetoric of American identity, and how the lynched black
body and the lynching photograph served as pedagogical texts that
inculcated citizens to the deep codes of American democracy. These
chapters illustrate how lynching has and continues to operate as a
state-sanctioned practice of reinscribing the color line in ways that
maintain the space of "the people"—that is, civic space—as space for
"whites only." In this chapter I examine how contemporary iterations of the lynching trope appearing during the 2008 and 2012 presidential elections reinscribed the us/them dialectic to demarcate the
White House and the Oval Office as space for whites only. Such performances, I argue, functioned as counterarguments to the advent
and continuance of a black presidency in ways that challenged the

notion of an America beyond race by demonstrating Americans' vested interest in a white racial state.

In 2004 Illinois senator Barack Obama made his national debut when he delivered the keynote speech for the Democratic National Convention. In the weeks preceding the 2008 and 2012 DNC presidential elections, lynched effigies of Obama populated white residential lawns and historically white university campuses. The lynching trope—particularly, the figure of the lynched black body—is a profoundly violent symbol of white citizenship belonging that signifies, among other things, the ultimate price blacks pay when they are believed to transgress the approved boundaries and precepts of their prescribed second-class status. In this chapter I examine how the advent of a black president troubled enclaves of white citizens who, in their inability to physically lynch Obama, took to lynching symbolic representations of Obama as a means of salving growing concern over the advent of black presidency.

Lynching in the age of Obama, like lynchings before, was about demarcating space for a certain kind of body. Of particular interest is how appeals to a white racial order articulated in contemporary reproductions of the lynching scene collapsed tropes of the black threat/enemy with those of the foreign invader to enthymematically demarcate the White House as space for "whites only" and Barack Obama as a threat to the sanctity and integrity of the nation. Such contemporary occasions resonate with a political and rhetorical tradition of antiblack violence while at the same time outing the fallacy of an America beyond race. Like *Without Sanctuary*'s recirculation of lynching imagery that reflected what white attitudes meant for blacks, so too did contemporary white citizens' symbolic lynching of America's first black president. My attention here to the symbolic lynching of America's first black presidential nominee, and later to the symbolic lynching of America's first black president, works to illustrate the ongoing purchase of lynching as an appeal to white solidarity and the ways antiblack sentiment is safely expressed by contemporary Americans who identify as members of the "citizen race."

"Fear of a Black President"

In 1993 Arkansas native Bill Clinton became the forty-second president of the United States. Clinton's cultural cachet—the fact that he was born poor, grew up in a single-parent household, played the saxophone, and reportedly felt "comfortable" in black communities—led some to agree with Toni Morrison that Clinton was America's "first black president." As Morrison explained, Bill Clinton's titular status had been granted long before her 1998 proclamation. Singer, songwriter, and Parliament Funkadelic leader George Clinton set the designation in motion with his 1993 release "Paint the White House Black." The song in a sense was an anthem to the president's projected ethos as a funk-loving, saxophone-playing, weed-smoking white boy from the South, an individual who, Morrison opined, displayed "almost every trope of blackness."[2] But Clinton's "blackness" was nominal, symbolic, and most importantly, complimentary. Regardless of the tribute, he remained meaningfully southern, phenotypically white, and thus an acceptable candidate for the White House. In 2004 discussions of a "black" White House resurfaced when Barack Obama, a young black Senate candidate from Illinois, delivered the keynote for the 2004 Democratic National Convention. Obama approached the stage as The Impressions' 1964 song, "Keep on Pushing" played in the background. He was casual but personable, engaging the crowd and giving shout-outs to his home states of Kansas, Illinois, and Hawaii. The audience roared. "Tonight is a particular honor for me," Obama began, "because let's face it, my presence on this stage is pretty unlikely."[3] The audience was silent.

Like the Oval Office, the DNC podium is a physical and historical space normed "white" through a network of rhetorically situated racial-spatial practices. Obama knew that the body his 2004 audience was expecting was not his body, and he unapologetically said as much when he punctuated his opening statement with just how "unlikely [his] presence on this stage" was. His candor communicated what those at the convention and those of us watching at home already knew, namely, that the DNC podium was envisioned as a certain kind of space intended for a certain kind of body that *was not* Obama's body.[4] The Impressions' 1964 hit, then, was more than catchy background music announcing the second African American since Barbara Jordan (1976) to occupy the DNC podium as keynote. Obama's declaration of the space behind the podium as space not intended for him illustrated an acute awareness of the rhetorical burden of being a black body in white space. His playful directive to "let's face it," quickly moved those at the convention and those watching at home from celebrating "diversity" as signified by the novelty of a black DNC keynote speaker, to implicating all in the truth that racial prejudice and racial injustice remain a shared reality of our time and an always already rhetorical constraint for not just Barack Hussein Obama, but all black members of the polity.

While Clinton's performance of blackness failed to impede his ascent to the Oval Office, both Obama's performance and his phenotypical blackness adversely impacted his. In 2007 Obama announced his candidacy for president, and as momentum gained, so too did challenges to the prospect of a black presidency. Joseph Lowndes reminds in his work on the representative and symbolic power of the presidency that presidents are "identifcatory figures" that "embody" and "emblemize" both what citizens hold dear and what they most despise.

> Presidential bodies become particularly salient when a new or counter-interpretation of national identity challenges the prevailing ones. These are often moments of inclusion—at least symbolically—of previously excluded groups. When such challenges occur, supporters in the electorate see themselves—and therefore the nation itself—in the figure of the president, in his physical being, his biography, his persona. Conversely, opponents of change project onto presidents or presidential candidates the negative aspects of the change they wish to halt.[5]

Projected onto Obama was fear of the nonwhite, non-Christian other. Bogus accusations contesting Obama's presidential bid constructed him presidentially "unfit" via fearmongering rhetoric that drew associations between his Muslim middle name "Hussein" and America's ongoing war against radical Islamic terrorists. Such discourse reiterating the links among whiteness, Americanness, and citizenship through tropes of the foreign, non-Christian invader constituted a discursive border that marked the White House as space for "whites only," and Obama too Muslim, too foreign and, thus, too un-American to be president.

Confusing Obama's name with Osama Bin Laden, one Philadelphia resident remarked, "I'm not sure of this, what's his name, Hussein Osama . . . Obama," but "There's no way I'll vote for him. I think he's a poser;"[6] even Republican competitor John McCain and Democrat and 2008 presidential opponent Hillary Clinton "othered" Obama through campaign ads that xenophobically referenced his middle name.[7] *Hardball*'s Chris Matthews instigatingly described Obama's middle name as "interesting," while others like *New York* magazine contributor Jennifer Senior—signifyin on the "unAmericanness" of Obama's international, multiracial, and multiethnic upbringing— cited his last name as the chief irony of an Obama presidency. In an article sardonically titled "Dreaming of Obama," Senior wrote,

> So much hope and so much fuss. All over a man whose father was from Kenya and whose mother might have been a distant relation of Jefferson Davis. Whose meals in Indonesia were served, for a time, by a male servant who sometimes liked to wear a dress. Whose first and last names *inconveniently* rhyme with "Iraq Osama." And whose middle name, taken from his Muslim grandfather, is, of all things, Hussein. Where else but here, though, right?[8]

Rhetorically "othering" Obama also included fearmongering rhetoric that outright denied Obama's status as a natural-born citizen, and xenophobic interpretations of black expressive culture. Whether it was a Kenyan-born Obama or an Indonesian-born Obama, birthers—named such on account of contesting Obama's

American birth—agreed that Obama could not be president because he was not a natural-born citizen. Congressmen, radio personalities and pundits fed white paranoia when they called for the release of Obama's birth certificate during the campaign. In June 2008 the Obama campaign responded by releasing his birth certificate and launching a fact-checking website that debunked these and other bogus allegations.[9]

The infamously misnamed "fist bump" shared later that month with wife Michelle just before Obama's 2008 victory speech provided further fodder for the pyre. The term "fist bump" aimed to describe an act of black camaraderie in practice since the 1960s. What black folks called "dap" or "pound" was a form of black communication, "a gesture of solidarity and comradeship" that as H. Samy Alim and Geneva Smitherman explain, is "also used in a celebratory sense and sometimes as a nuanced greeting among intimates and/or those with a shared social history."[10] Obama reiterated as much during an interview with NBC's Brian Williams following his 2008 nomination victory in St. Paul. Describing the exchange, he said, "It captured what I love about my wife—there's an irreverence about her and sense that for all the hoopla, that I'm her husband and sometimes we'll do silly things. She's proud of me and she gives me some credit once in a while, but I actually pull some things off."[11] The Obamas' performance of blackness as black bodies on a national stage troubled those committed to a white worldview. What Fox News host E. D. Hill zealously described as a "terrorist fist jab" was exacerbated by the *New Yorker*'s July 2008 "The Politics of Fear" cover parodying the incident.[12] The visual rhetoric of the *New Yorker* cover personified the rhetorical border of anti-Obamaist discourse through its depiction of the White House as a space invaded by black anti-American—that is, anti-white—anticitizens. The image of an army fatigue wearing, afro-sprouting, machine-gun-carrying Michelle and a turban-wearing Barack giving dap in an Oval Office adorned with a framed picture of Osama Bin Laden and a burning American flag depicted the soon-to-be First Couple as two halves of an equally problematic whole. Obama supporters denounced the cover as "tasteless and offensive," "trash," and "disgusting."[13] But as artist Barry Britt explained, "the idea that the Obamas are branded as unpatriotic [let alone as terrorists] in certain sectors is preposterous. It seemed to me that depicting the concept would show it as the fear-mongering ridiculousness that it is."[14]

Despite the absence of a physical sign, America's long history of racially demarcating space—Indian laws, slave codes, black codes, anti- miscegenation laws, voter registration laws, anti-immigration laws, and Jim Crow (most notably designated via "Whites Only" signs) among other exclusionary decrees—definitively figured the White House and the Oval Office as "whites only" spaces. The 2008 election further evidenced this reality, demonstrating that in an era "beyond race," blacks enacting their right to jockey for the historically white space of America's Oval Office were, just as during segregation, delegitimized, defamed, warned to stay in their place and, finally, with the threat of transgressing the color line at its greatest, lynched. Oftentimes the safest option for bodies lacking the privilege of being the somatic norm is to find creative ways of mitigating white imaginings of "the dangerous trespasser" while maintaining a sense of self-respect.

In his essay "Just Walk on By," journalist Brent Staples illustrates that negotiating damaging stereotypes such as the foreigner, "black threat," "black mugger," and other contemporary versions of the mythologized black beast, takes a dynamic understanding of the relationships between whiteness, race, and space. While walking through the physically and historically white spaces of northside Chicago, SoHo, and parts of Brooklyn, Staples whistles selections from Antonio Vivaldi's *Four Seasons* as a way of signaling familiarity. Whistling "melodies from Beethoven and Vivaldi and the more popular classical composers" helps Staples safely navigate these white spaces by reducing the tension that arises when his six-foot-two black body is perceived to be out of place. Staples's dilemma is a condition of always already being surveilled, evaluated, and deemed

Figure 4.1. Barry Blitt, "The Politics of Fear," *New Yorker*, July 21, 2008. Courtesy of Barry Blitt/The New Yorker. © Conde Nast.

vile on account of being black and male. Whistling Vivaldi may not stop the "click" of locking car doors that rings out as Staples crosses the street but, when deployed in closer proximities, can help ease white paranoia and its resulting potential for black death. Classical music is a marker of culture not typically associated with blackness or the danger assumed to come with blackness. He explains, "Virtually everybody seems to sense that a mugger wouldn't be warbling bright, sunny selections" of classical music while walking down the street.[15] And it is here that Staples illustrates his connection to the devastating reality that his safety as a black man walking in spaces designated white is determined by his ability to mediate the stereotypes associated with his body, stereotypes that his white counterparts may or may not consciously hold but the consequences of which he may indefinitely suffer. While Staples's account speaks to how his black male body operates within the white imaginary as a symbolic of danger, the reactions he receives from white passersby— the looks of suspicion, the siccing of dogs, the clicking of car door locks, and the efforts to avoid him—elucidate that Staples's life is predicated upon his capacity to mitigate the white racist stereotypes associated with his body. His reports of the noticeable difference between the attitudes of white passersby for whom he whistles and those he does not testify to how strategic deployment of tropes of whiteness may help to make bodies marked "foreign" familiar.

Whistling Vivaldi

The presidency constitutes a rhetorical situation that presented a particularly unique set of constraints for Obama, who, on account of his blackness, could not outright ignore it. He was compelled by the exigency of the presidency to present himself as "fit" for the historically white role of commander-in-chief and the historically white space of the Oval Office by cohering with the collective imagining citizens have of the president. As communications scholar Keith Erickson explains, citizens' "perceptions of the office demand that a president act presidential with such palpable authenticity as to display 'true performance,'" which "constitutes a prudent adaptation to the standards and traditions of the presidency."[16] To be presidential is to be poised, measured, firm but fair, judicious, sincere, and phenotypically white. To cohere with his audience's imaginings of the president, Obama must mediate the signifying power of his blackness while affirming *"visual mastery of the mythic presidency."* [17] Visually mastering the presidency, however, is difficult for a body ideologically conceived devoid of the moral virtue requisite for the presidency. If the performance, which includes the physical appearance, tone, and tenor of the rhetor, does not stamp him or her as authentically presidential in the eyes of the audience, then the speaker fails.[18]

In March 2008 Obama exhibited the poise and judiciousness that constitute a prudent presidential character when he addressed questions regarding then–spiritual advisor Rev. Jeremiah Wright's allegedly anti-American sermons. Delivered at the National Constitution Center in Philadelphia, the speech titled "A More Perfect Union" was widely praised, and subsequently deemed Obama "quintessentially American" and "presidential," and the prospect of his presidency one that could potentially bring America's divided nation closer to reconciliation.[19] The speech was in response to yet another attempt to reiterate the links among whiteness, Americanness, and citizenship. Earlier that March a smear campaign circulated doctored clips of Wright's "inflammatory" sermons as "evidence" of Obama's radicalism. Rather than chastise the media for its perpetuation of "nasty politics as usual" or deliver an apologia meant to recuperate what some described as a damaged ethos,[20] Obama, exuding even tone and composure, and refusing to further contribute to the political fodder by apologizing for Wright's statements, instead collapsed public memory of America's "legacy of discrimination" and bootstraps tradition to contextualize Wright's representation of "black anger" and the mainstream media's representation of "white resentment" as symptoms of America's "unfinished" objective of true democracy.[21]

We can dismiss Reverend Wright as a crank or a demagogue. . . . But race is an issue that I believe this nation cannot afford to ignore right now. We would be making the same mistake that Reverend Wright made in his offending sermons about America—to simplify and stereotype and amplify the negative to the point that it distorts reality. The fact that the comments that have been made and the issues that have surfaced over the last few weeks reflect the complexities of race in this country that we've never really worked through—a part of our union that we have yet to perfect. . . . Understanding this reality requires a reminder of how we arrived at this point . . . [we] need to remind ourselves that so many of the disparities that exist in the African-American community today can be directly traced to inequalities passed on from an earlier generation that suffered under the brutal legacy of slavery and Jim Crow. . . . Just as black anger often proved counterproductive, so have . . . white resentments distracted attention from the real culprits of the middle class squeeze—a corporate culture rife with inside dealing, questionable accounting practices, and short-term greed; a Washington dominated by lobbyists and special interests; economic policies that favor the few over the many. And yet, to wish away the resentments of white Americans, to label them as misguided or even racist, without recognizing they are grounded in legitimate concerns—this too widens the racial divide and blocks the path to understanding. This is where we are right now. It's a racial stalemate we've been stuck in for years. Contrary to the claims of some of my critics, black and white, I have never been so naive as to believe that we can get beyond our racial divisions in a single election cycle, or with a single candidacy—particularly a candidacy as imperfect as my own.[22]

"A More Perfect Union" exhibited a rhetorical adeptness for managing the burdens of the mythic presidency. Balance is a political necessity for presidents, and here Obama performed the presidency by appearing informed (via a historicization that contextualizes the fodder) and impartial (via a refusal to choose sides) while simultaneously sympathetic to the frustrations and plights of Americans across the color line. What some have criticized as pandering, however, is considered here to be Obama's rendition of "whistling Vivaldi." Whiteness is an ideological code that haunts both physical and discursive space.[23] Like all white racialized spaces, the presidency is composed of a set of orthodoxies—accepted views, expectations, attitudes, and practices—that have been, through invariable repetition—what we might call, *tradition*—calcified so flawlessly that they express as commonsense, natural, and standard as opposed to constructed. These racialized norms and hierarchies create racialized expectations for "the people" as well as racialized rhetorical constraints for citizens such as Obama who lack the privileges of white racial standing. Deviating from these expectations would be to lose the presidency. Consequently, the rhetorical constraints of a phenotypically black presidential candidate mean that to appear partial to blacks or to articulate—or be perceived as articulating—a "pro-black" stance would be to lose the presidency. Additionally, failure to legitimate the anger and frustrations of both blacks and whites, the hopes of both, and to identify responsibility for America's current "racial stalemate" as both black and white would be to lose the presidency. Whistling Vivaldi here—that is, mitigating white fears over his perceived militancy—means that Obama must strike a balance between the public's expectations of presidential prudence and historical imaginings of the black threat. The ability to parse out with poise and in simple language the looming impact of racist ideology for both whites and blacks in a presumably post-racial society, and to use the memory of that shared past of racial inegalitarianism to at once acknowledge Americans' "different stories" while at the same time redirecting attention towards "common hopes," was characteristically presidential in its diplomacy, paternalism, and advocacy for unity. Rhetoric racializes all bodies, as such; Obama's whistling does not reflect a mode of discursively "passing for white" as much as it illustrates the political need to calibrate his performance according to the rhetorical constraints of the US presidency.

"A More Perfect Union" was an instance in which Obama molli-fied anxiety over a diminishing white ideal by performing the presi-dency with visual authenticity. Such a move intimates that the issue at hand commands the respect of direct face-to-face address while at the same time granting Obama the opportunity to visually per-form the presidency by addressing "the people" on a national prob-lem. Presidents are tasked with the responsibility of addressing the nation during times of turmoil and devastation. In calling a national press conference, Obama invoked a level of presidential authority that cohered with collective imaginings of the president as the peo-ple's steward and commander-in-chief. A live national address con-jures a sense of urgency through its call for the immediate attention of all citizens. A live address also implies the willingness to be seen and visually verified in real time. The symbolic significance of the speech site as well as the optics of the occasion also assisted Obama's construction of presidential prudence. Although not the Oval Office, the Constitutional Center is the only nonpartisan institution estab-lished by Congress to educate citizens about the US Constitution. As such, it served as the premier site for an address that called upon "the people" to honor the spirit of their shared ideals. This location and the visual rhetoric of Obama's black body positioned between two large American flags as he delivered a message of racial reconcilia-tion against a backdrop of patriotic blue, framed America's soon-to-be first black presidential nominee as a man fit to lead the nation.

"One of Us"

Presidential qualities are normatively applied to white male bodies because the position of commander-in-chief of the United States of America has been, for the last 232 years, the exclusive purview of white men. In addition to addresses like "A More Perfect Union," which helped Obama cohere with collective imaginings of the presi-dent, staged performance fragments like those operating during the 2008 DNC Convention likewise reified the notion that Obama, despite looking like one of "them" was actually one of "us."

On the last night of the convention, Obama's acceptance speech was preceded by Dick Durbin's keynote, which included verbal remarks and a documentary video narrating Obama's life story and political ascent. Speaking as the representative stand-in for "we the people," Durbin declared, "So many of us know this man. We know how he thinks. We know his values. We know Barack Obama's journey has never been far from the pain and struggles so many Americans experience today."[24] "We" know that Obama, is "one of us," asserted Durbin, because we have judged him by the content of his character as opposed to the color of his skin. Such framing added veracity to the documentary's depiction of Obama as a man the people could trust. Durbin's rhetorical embodiment of "the people" through use of the plural "we" helped to counter the fearmongering rhetoric that constructed Obama as an outsider, other, and threat to the nation.

Deploying national memory of Illinois senator and eleventh president Abraham Lincoln likewise assisted Durbin's depiction of Obama as a man familiar to "us." In his address the fellow Illinois senator described Obama as the "other son of Illinois."[25] If national memory figures Lincoln as the nation's savior, then casting America's first black presidential nominee as the second coming invites the audience to infer that Obama's presidency will give birth to a new nation. This and other allusions to Lincoln followed suit with Obama's own efforts to rhetorically figure himself "Lincolnesque" and thus as a man both familiar and well suited for the presidency. Obama did this during the 2004 DNC keynote when he used the memory of Lincoln to cast himself as a sagacious, even-tempered, civic-minded, ethical, and balanced politician. He did it again when he selected the front of the Illinois capitol building (the same place where Lincoln spoke 150 years ago) to announce his candidacy for president,[26] and he would do it again while giving his 2008 inaugural speech. Durbin's allusion contin-

ued Obama's strategy of troping Lincoln by framing Obama within
a narrative of messianic deliverance, that cast him as a man des-
tined to bring salvation to a people tired of division. With Obama's
election, Durbin asserted, comes the "dawning of a new day," for he
would, like Lincoln, "lead us to a better nation."

Durbin's strategic use of national memory helps to mitigate the
adverse effects of Obama's racialized body by strengthening the
audience's focus on the ways in which Obama—despite his signifiers
of blackness—embodies fundamental principles of Americanness.
Through Durbin, Americans at the convention and watching at home
were brought to see that Obama's personal story was a part of "the
larger American story." The documentary that aired later continued
Durbin's efforts by first invoking classic narratives of the American
Dream. The film opens with scenic shots of the American Midwest
from a bus. Expansive panoramas of wheat fields and cornfields pass
by as the bus hurtles onward. It is against this backdrop that viewers
see Obama interacting with representations of "the people" depicted
as farmers and blue-collar workers of the American Midwest. These
performance frames depict Obama out among "the people," shaking hands with "the people," listening intently as "the people" speak
to him, and laughing with "the people." The video quickly moves
from the heartland of Obama's upbringing to the Midwest city of his
political ascent. Pictures of a young Obama as a grassroots organizer
in Chicago are accompanied by testimonies to his character as an
ethical and vivacious civic leader. Congressmen describe Obama as
the archetypal public servant. He is a man "compelled to serve" to the
benefit and improved welfare of all citizens. As Illinois state senator Miguel del Valle explains, Obama's Ivy League education doesn't
detach him from understanding the "day-to-day" troubles of the
average American: unemployment, "factory closings," low-wage pay,
and "failing schools." Illinois senator Laurence M. Walsh confirmed
Obama's integrity: "Pieces of legislation that he carried he believed
in," Walsh affirmed. "He was not carrying it for a group; he was not
carrying it for a lobbyist." These performance frames paint Obama

as a man whose politics are grounded in fundamental American values and interests: economic freedom, educational equality, personal liberty, and equal employment. Such frames help Obama perform citizens' imaginings of the presidency by figuring him as the embodiment of core democratic principles.

The visual and verbal rhetoric of the documentary also affirms Durbin's construction of Obama as "one of us" through performance frames that rhetorically whiten Obama. The video achieves this by stressing Obama's "Americanness" through signifiers of whiteness. The abundance of performance frames depicting Obama living and working comfortably alongside professional, political, and suit-wearing whites, elderly whites, white grandparents, his white mother, whites in hardhats, and whites in long white smocks, impresses upon viewers that although often the only black body in the frame, Obama nonetheless seems to belong in the frame. Such displays uphold "the people's" racialized expectations of the president as a man who moves comfortably in all spaces as it depicts Obama as a black man who moves comfortably in spaces both inundated by white bodies and historically inaccessible to blacks. The video likewise uses the story of Obama's upbringing—specifically, the story of his bloodline and family origins—to depict him as devoutly "American." Although Obama was not a serviceman himself, his roots are patriotic in that his white grandparents and primary caretakers served in World War II: his grandfather as a serviceman and his grandmother as a worker on a bomber assembly line. In the documentary Obama describes his grandparents Stanley and Madelyn Dunham as "hardworking" people of America's "heartland." "They weren't complainers.....[T]hey took life as it came." Depicting his grandparents and primary caretakers as exemplary American patriots figures Obama a product of their bootstrap and loyalist mentality.

While the documentary depicts Obama's maternal grandparents as a self-reliant, patriotic couple that taught Obama the importance of hard work, it portrayed his mother, Stanley Anne Dunham, as his moral compass. She was the "beating heart" of a very small family,

Obama reflected. In the documentary Obama explains that it was his mother's lessons in fairness, empathy, and equality that guided his desire to pursue a life of civil service.

> The only time I saw my mother really angry was when she saw cruelty, when she saw somebody being bullied or somebody being treated differently because of who they were. And if she saw me doing that, she would be furious. And she would say to me: "Imagine standing in that person's shoes; how would that make you feel?" That simple idea I'm not always sure I understood as a kid, but it stayed with me.[27]

Obama's later admission in the documentary to having been "shaped more by [his African] father's *absence* than his presence" strengthens Durbin's confirmation of Obama's Americanness by confirming his relative distance from blackness during his formative years (emphasis added). Narrating Obama's upbringing as absent black influence and rich in American—that is, white—mores is a visual and narrative strategy intended to mitigate the rhetorical constraints associated with Obama's black body.

Lynching Obama

That October following the 2008 DNC Convention rhetorical enactments racially demarcating the White House as space for whites only manifested in the form of lynched Obama effigies. Like the figure of the lynching victim during the early nineteenth century, lynched effigies of America's first black presidential candidate were used to racially demarcate the White House as the sole and exclusive purview of citizens with white racial standing. At the Newberg, Oregon, Christian college George Fox, four students erected a life-size cardboard effigy of Obama and hung it from a tree. The historically white institution holds a religious charge to produce students that are both academically and spiritually prepared to perform their professional lives with passion and integrity.[28] The reenactment underscored the religiosity of lynching among Christian communities that conceived such performances as a powerful ritual of purification and community renewal in which God considered the brutal aggression enacted against victims to be consecrate.[29] Particular to the students' reenactment was the "Act Six Reject" sign attached to the front of the effigy. Act Six was a George Fox scholarship program aimed at increasing campus diversity.[30] While symbolically lynching such a student was an act of community that reaffirmed who did and who did not belong at George Fox, favoring such a student after America's first black presidential candidacy and lynching him just shy of the 2008 November election placed George Fox students squarely within America's tradition of civic belonging.

On October 18, 2008, Ohio business owner Mike Lunsford lynched a white-sheeted ghost from a tree on his front lawn that had a sign supporting McCain and Palin's 2008 campaign anchored in the ground below it. Attached upside down to the front of the effigy was a sign on which Obama's middle name was spray-painted and misspelled. Lunsford, who spoke to a Cincinnati news reporter off camera for fear that his political views would hurt his employees, candidly pronounced his racism. He explained that he was against the idea of an "African American running the country," that Obama was not a "full-blooded American," and that he believed America was a "white Christian nation and that only white Christians should be in power."[31] Lunsford's anti-Obama rhetoric echoed that of segregationists and white supremacists whose appeals to white democracy turned on claims of racial degradation, founders' intent, and white rights. According to Lunsford, if America was a white Christian nation to be run by white Christian men, then sanctioning the categorical other as leader of the free world was to undo the very notion of America. Lynching Obama, then, permitted Lunsford to safeguard the nation while at the same time permitting him to reaffirm his identity as a member of the "citizen race." The Obama effigy, then, like Joe's postcard photograph of William Stanley's lynching, is Lunsford's pledge to a white racial

Figure 4.2. Kirk Deddo's front lawn Obama effigy. Clarksville, Indiana. October 2008.

Figure 4.3. Mike Lunsford's Obama effigy. Fairfield, Ohio. October 2008

state, his performance of white solidarity, and his endorsement of white democracy.

That same month two students at the University of Kentucky were arrested for lynching an Obama effigy on campus, while a Redondo Beach, California, woman was ordered to remove her effigy that featured a butcher knife in Obama's neck.[32] In both instances culprits exhibited historical amnesia when criticized and sanctioned over the racist nature of their displays. In the Redondo Beach incident, the owner deflected accusations of racism by claiming that her display was simply a Halloween decoration. Legal counsel for Kentucky students Joe Fischer and Hunter Bush stated that the effigy the boys displayed on campus was not racist but rather "an ill-conceived political prank" for which the charges of burglary, theft, and disorderly conduct were "very extreme."[33] Kirk Deddo in Clarksville, Indiana, similarly sought to save face when he received criticism over the Obama effigy hanging from a tree in his front lawn. Deddo maintained that his life-size Halloween decoration was not racist but political, explaining that he couldn't think of anything scarier than the prospect of Obama leading the country.[34] While the rhetoric of Deddo's verbal defense left the nature of his fear unstated, the trope of the black lynching victim manifest in his rendition of the Obama effigy enthymematically communicated what Deddo believed to be the best way to manage white fear over a black presidency.

Conclusion

The rhetorical border contesting Obama's candidacy reiterated the link between citizenship and whiteness; so too did lynched Obama effigies. The heightened presence of Obama effigies as Obama's triumph grew near invoked a time when objection to the full inclusion of blacks within America's political imaginary produced a strange and bitter fruit. In the case of Obama, enactments of white citizenship were united by a discourse of antiblackness that forwarded an appeal to white racial rule by collapsing tropes of the black threat/enemy with those of the foreign invader to enthymematically demarcate, by way of the Obama effigy, that the White House was a space for whites only. Claims defending these displays as "political" as opposed to "racist" utilized the false logic that politics and race are mutually exclusive. Race is by its very definition political. What Obama effigies communicated, then, was that a black candidate of mixed-race heritage, the product of an open and public interracial union—specifically, the union of a white woman and a black African man—who had in the eyes of those committed to a white ideal come to lay claim to what had been since the nation's inception the political birthright of whites, was a man firmly "out of place." Obama effigies enthymematically racializing space through visual tropes of white civic belonging replaced mid twentieth-century signs of legalized segregation reading "No Blacks Allowed." Despite the absence of a burning torch, volleys of bullets, a dismembered body, or even a raging crowd (although the media frenzy that these incidents created is tantamount to such an audience), the symbolic lynching of a black man who has been seen—in some shape, way, or form—as one who has transgressed his prescribed "place," suggests that lynching today continues to retain the same civic resonance it did in the past. Symbolically lynching Obama offered these citizens a double victory, then, in that it both granted the opportunity to salve what ailed them by reclaiming the racialized space of the White House as the exclusive space of "whites only" and ensured the maintenance of a white ideal during a time of political uncertainty.

CONCLUSION

A CIVIC LESSON CONTINUED

When black bodies are objectified by white gazes, reduced to
surfaces, and stereotyped, this too is a species of the color line
being drawn.[1]
—GEORGE YANCY, *Look, a White!*

In 2012 Barack Obama claimed yet another historic victory when
he became the first African American to win a second presidential
term. That election, like the one before it, was equally plagued by
discourse that reiterated the link between whiteness, Americanness,
and citizenship. Signs demanding Obama return to Kenya and signs
asserting communist leanings circulated campaign rallies, social
media, and local billboards as the 2012 election gained traction. In
a local town just outside of Boston, motorcycle accessories distribu-
tor Robert Sullivan displayed a billboard of the 2012 Democratic
presidential candidate with hammer-and-sickle lapel pins that read,
"Somewhere in Kenya, a village is missing its idiot. Obama, One Big
Ass Mistake for America. Vote Mitt Romney for President." Across
from it was another billboard sponsored by Sullivan showcasing a
little white girl with blonde hair and an exaggeratedly sad face giving Obama the finger and calling him a "jerk" for his lack of fiscal
conservatism.[2] These ads depicting Obama as inept and ineffectual

turned on preexisting tropes of black incompetence in ways that both implicitly and explicitly asserted that to vote for a black man during the 2012 election was to vote against America's best interests. Racist bumper stickers, pins, and hats bearing slogans like "Don't Renig 2012" and "NøBAMA," and T-shirts advocating that Americans "Put the White Back in the White House," framed Obama's blackness as a chief problem of his candidacy. No performance of the 2012 election communicated this more than "chair lynchings." This iteration of the lynching trope utilizing empty chairs was inspired by Clint Eastwood's 2012 Republican National Convention speech, in which he hurled criticisms at an empty chair meant to symbolize a lazy, absent, and ineffectual Obama. "He doesn't go to work. He doesn't go down to Congress and make a deal. What the hell's he doing sitting in the White House? If I were in that job, I'd get down there and make a deal. Sure, Congress are lazy bastards, but so what? You're the top guy."[3]

In the weeks that followed, supporters adapted Eastwood's empty chair speech to more familiarly sadistic ends. What a Centerville, Virginia, man referred to as "Eastwooding," then, included hanging a chair with the sign "NOBAMA" attached to it.[4] Eighty miles outside of Minneapolis in Kasson, Minnesota, Laura Mulholland embellished her empty chair by thrusting a bayonet through it.[5] Another display in Austin, Texas, included an American flag. As with the Obama effigies in 2008, the 2012 chair-lynching enthusiasts constructed a narrative of white innocence through a rhetoric of colorblindness that denied the racist intent of their displays.[6] Colorblind rhetoric defends and perpetuates the contemporary racial order through interpretive frames that normalize racism. In the case of chair lynchings, enthusiasts denied the racist sentiment of their performances by framing them as part of a liberal democratic tradition. In the case of Centerville resident Doug Burger, denying the racist intent of his chair-lynching display, began by first conceding to the racially motivated nature of lynching. Affirming the racist symbolism of the noose, Burger rejoined, "I am not a racist in any fashion . . . I know how to build a noose, really. If I wanted to make a noose, I could do that. I did not. I had no intention for that to occur." Following Burger's logic, his use of a knot (which holds things in place) compared to a noose (which, keeping with the context of his response, is used to execute blacks) rendered his 2012 chair display clean of racist intent. Sealing his innocence, Burger concluded that his motivation for hanging the display was to keep it from vandals.[7]

Bud Johnson, who on the other hand was quite irate over local criticism, feigned outrage over what he described as "stupid" people attacking his right to free speech. Of the lynched chair on his front lawn, he insisted, "It's not a lynch . . . It's the only place I had to put up the goddamn thing!" So, "No, it has no other meaning!"[8] Here, Burger constructed white innocence through language that framed protest over his display as ignorant. As he implied, only the uninformed and poorly educated would be so "stupid" as to assume that his display was a "lynch."[9] The Maxwells of Washington state employed a similar discursive strategy. Their iterations of the lynching trope included an empty chair hanging from a tree with a sign below it that read, "ARE YOU BETTER OFF NOW THAN 4 YEARS AGO? The King is A Joke." At one point the display included a "NOBAMA" sign and two American flags. When contacted by reporters Kathryn Maxwell exclaimed, "Oh dear . . . The reason we hung it up was because people kept stealing it . . . We just have to take extra precautions." While Johnson and others eventually removed their displays, the Maxwells refused on the grounds of constitutional right. Referencing the right to free speech, "There's a Constitution," Kathryn Maxwell said. "Some people forget that."[10]

In the case of chair lynchings, offenders assumed a postracial sensibility by asserting a pragmatic and civic reason for their displays. Burger's display was not racist because it did not display a noose, and Johnson's and Maxwell's displays were not racist because the constitutional right to free speech is not racist. Such moments of rhetorically saving face continue a discourse of white citizenship via colorblind displays of what contemporary proponents of a white

Figure 5.1. "Centerville Man Says Lynching Not Implied by Hanging 'Nobama' Chair from Tree," Virginia, WJLA Washington, D.C., September 20, 2012.

democracy collectively refer to as "political protest." Consequently, these individuals are not racist, but rather simply active partici-pants of democratic society; their effigies are racially benign modes of healthy civic engagement. In each case, flipping accusations of racism into misinterpretations of intent constructed a narrative of white innocence that allowed citizens invested in a white ideal to feign colorblindness by denying the racist intention of their actions.[11]

Figure 5.2. "Is This an Anti-Obama Lynching? Texas Man Hangs Chair from Tree Inspired by Clint Eastwood Speech." Texas New York Daily News, September 21, 2012.

Just as lynched effigies of Obama symbolically delineated the imagined and physical space of the presidency as a space solely for whites, so too did chair lynchings. Chair lynchings, like the spectacle lynchings from which they derived, were forms of racist intimidation that contested the ways constitutional amendments had empowered Obama to enact the full extent of his civic sensibility. Lynching him, then, was part of a longer rhetorical tradition in which white figurations of the black body in peril championed the continuance of a white supremacy.

No Retreat: Emmett Till "Over and Over Again"

On February 26, 2012, less than a month into Obama's second presidency, seventeen-year-old Trayvon Martin was shot and killed in the predominantly white gated community called the Retreat; he was returning home from 7-11 with snacks for his little brother. On July 11, 2013, a jury of six women, all white save one Latina, found George Zimmerman, the self-appointed neighborhood patrolman of the Retreat, not guilty in the killing of Trayvon Martin. That evening Obama offered condolences to Trayvon's parents, while at the same time calling for national restraint over the verdict. Synthesizing Trayvon's body as a body he himself inhabited and as a body he himself could seed, Obama remarked, "Trayvon . . . could have been my son. Another way of saying that is Trayvon Martin could have been me thirty-five years ago."[12] The statement asserted that while things had changed, much had within the last thirty-five years stayed the same. As Obama explained, Trayvon's surveillance, accusation, and subsequent killing, and the acquittal of his killer, echoed a "very difficult history" of institutionalized racial disparity that contextualized how African Americans interpreted the trial.[13]

The "very difficult history" Obama avoided detailing included America's history of lynching. Those outraged at the verdict read continuity between the logic and discourse used to legitimate Trayvon's killing and the logic and discourse that legitimated lynching. The incident carried classic tropes of the lynching scene and lynching narrative. Zimmerman was never arrested. Sanford police filed the incident as self-defense, following Florida's notorious "Stand Your Ground" law, which removes citizens' duty to retreat from bodily harm or the perceived threat of bodily harm by permitting them to pursue perceived assailants with deadly force. Under this law, Zimmerman was permitted to assume a historically "white right" to kill with impunity. Second, the trial that ensued sought to protect Zimmerman's right to kill by perpetuating stereotypes of the black beast threat. As the defense asserted, the killing of Trayvon Martin was not an act of racism, but rather a consequence of mistaken identity. Had Trayvon not donned an emblem of black criminality—that is, a hoodie—had he not had his hands in his pockets, and had he not evaded Zimmerman (because he felt threatened), then Zimmerman would have never had a reason to fear for his life. Third, the defense deployed tropes of the black beast rapist by juxtaposing the image of a white female resident of the Retreat with an image of a shirtless, "thugged-out version" of Trayvon. Casting Trayvon as a thug contested the notion of an "innocent" boy through imagery that "adultified" him, criminalized him, and resounded with justifications given for lynching in the way it changed the narrative from "Zimmerman the racist killer" to "Zimmerman the chivalrous hero protecting white women and the white community from black threats." Inviting the jury to perceive Trayvon's intent via visual tropes of white innocence and black criminality rhetorically whitened and—as a benefit of this whitening—expunged Zimmerman's culpability by, as the *Nation*'s Mychal Denzel Smith remarked, "literally invok[ing] the same justification for the killing of Trayvon Martin that you would during lynching."[14] Melanie Morrison, executive director of the social justice network Allies of Change, observed similarly, noting that the "lack of identification" between jurors and Trayvon was rooted "in the legacies of lynching that continue to infect white Americans."[15] It was this history, explained journalist Isabel Wilkerson, that generated a "lack in empathy" that allowed jurors to disidentify with "the plight of [a] fellow citize[n]."[16]

According to Karen Johnson and Kenneth Johnson, Trayvon's slaying read "familiar to generations of African Americans," because they "have witnessed these types of tragedies for centuries."[17] Trayvon's killing and Zimmerman's acquittal reminded many of an era that America had supposedly surpassed. As actress Angela Bassett testified, "The Trayvon Martin case in Florida adds another name to the terrible legacy of young black men like . . . Emmett Till."[18] Along with Emmett, Bassett called on the memories of Oscar Grant, the unarmed black man gunned down by Oakland police in 2009, and Amadou Diallo, who in 1999 was killed in a rain of forty-one police bullets as evidence of a changing same. According to reports, the officer who killed Grant meant to Tase him after he'd already been restrained but "inadvertently" killed him when he accidently pulled out his gun instead. In the case of Diallo, police surrounded

and opened fire after "mistaking" Diallo for a man officers had
arrested days earlier. Bassett's mosaic of antiblack policing read the
past and present as one to assert, like others, that America's predilec-
tion for lynching had not been cured but had simply taken another
form. In an email, the chairperson of the NAACP National Board of
Directors, Roslyn Brock, asserted similarly: "In 1955, a young black
man in Money, Mississippi, went to the store to buy some candy.
Fifty-seven years later, another black man in Sanford, Florida, did
the same. Both trips led to a death—one of Emmett Till and the
other Trayvon Martin."[19] Trayvon's killing "spoke to a long history of
'profiling,' where Black subjectivity is read, named and acted upon in
the context of a civil democratic society."[20]

Black citizens read continuity between the 1955 lynching of
Emmett Louis Till and the killing of Trayvon Martin in part because
the conditions of both incidents mirrored so closely. To start, both
boys were black teens: Emmett was fourteen and Trayvon was sev-
enteen; both were visitors to the places they were killed: Emmett was
visiting family in Mississippi, and Trayvon was visiting his father;
both boys failed to comply with the racial order, and neither boy
whistled Vivaldi—that is, neither youth enacted tropes of whiteness to mitigate the consequences of being presumed a body "out
of place." Second, both Trayvon and Emmett died after going to the
local store: Emmett was tracked down and murdered after buying
candy at the Bryants' shop, and Trayvon was tracked down and killed
after a 7-11 run for iced tea and a bag of Skittles. Third, both slayings
were united by acts of contest in which both boys rebuffed the white
gaze of the men who lynched them. In the exposé with *Look* magazine, Milam described Emmett as defiant in part because he refused
to be seen the way Milam saw him. Similarly, the struggle that
ensued before the fatal shot and Rachael Jeantel's testimony during
Zimmerman's trial suggested that Trayvon likewise rejected the racist gaze of the lyncher. Rachael, who was on the phone with Trayvon
during his encounter with Zimmerman, testified that Trayvon "kept
complaining that a man was just watching him [. . . .] that this creepy
[explicative] cracker" was following him.[21] Conceiving Zimmerman's

Figure 5.3. J. Gonzalez-Blitz, "Emmett Till & Trayvon Martin 1955–2013." Courtesy of J. Gonzalez-Blitz.

actions as "creepy" categorized his presumed authority to look and judge with impunity as strange, suspicious, and illegitimate. As the 911 transcript illustrated, Zimmerman's account of the moment he and Trayvon first exchanged looks speaks more to an underlying agitation with how his efforts to oversee the teen were spurned, as opposed to his reported fear of Trayvon's presence.

911-DISPATCHER: Did you see what he was wearing?

ZIMMERMAN: Yeah, a dark hoodie like a gray hoodie. He wore jeans or sweat pants and white tennis shoes. He's here now . . . he's just staring. [00:42]

911-DISPATCHER: He's just walking around the area, the houses? OK.
ZIMMERMAN: Now he's staring at me. [00:48] [. . . .] Uh, huh. Something's wrong with him. Yep, he's coming to check me out. He's
got something in his hands. I don't know what his deal is [01:20]
911-DISPATCHER: We've got him on the wire. Just let me know if this
guy does anything else.
ZIMMERMAN: OK. These assholes. They always get away . . . [1:39]
[. . . .] He's running. [2:08] [. . . .] [It sounds like Zimmerman
says under his breath "F-ing coons" at 02:22][22]

The parallels follow in that like Milam, Zimmerman is notably per-
turbed when narrating the moment Trayvon acknowledges being
overseen. Lastly, the deaths of both boys galvanized social movements
in which both were dubbed sacrificial lambs—Emmett the sacrificial
lamb of the civil rights movement, and Trayvon the sacrificial lamb
of the Movement for Black Lives. Such eerily akin conditions anchor-
ing Trayvon's killing in the memory of Emmett Till made it easy to
see why many read Trayvon and Emmett as "the same thing."[23]

Christopher Benson, coauthor of *Death of Innocence* with the late
Mamie Till-Mobley, metonymically constructed more recent incidents of antiblack violence as iterations of Emmett's lynching when
he explained Emmett's power as a representative anecdote.[24]

When we see the case of Trayvon Martin or Michael Brown or Tamir
Rice, where young Black males are shot down by authority figures
and nobody's punished, it reminds us of the most celebrated case
where a Black teen was killed and nobody was brought to justice. . . .
It is no wonder, then, that each time we read about another young
unarmed black male being shot down in the street—unjustly—by
any authority figure, there is the mention of Emmett's name.[25]

As Benson explains here, the name and memory of Emmett Till
summate a pattern of experience evidencing the precariousness of
black life in America—more specifically, the precariousness of black

boyhood in America. Within the political vocabulary of black citizens, Emmett serves as a representative anecdote reflecting a race-critical and race-conscious understanding of how and why justice and democracy evade black citizens. If we concede that incidents of antiblack police brutality and antiblack vigilante justice such as this one are reverberations of a past not passed, then we recognize how the metonymical construction of Trayvon Martin as Emmett Till is part of a longer tradition of communicating America's ways and, in the words of Trudier Harris, urging blacks to identify with what those ways have meant in terms of destruction for them.[26]

Wages of White Citizenship

Zimmerman's assumed right to police Trayvon—specifically, his demand that Trayvon legitimate his presence inside the gated community of the Retreat by verifying his presence with its self-appointed guardian—turned on a long history of overseeing and overdetermining the black body as "out of place." From freedom papers to labor contracts to library cards and driver's licenses, blacks have historically been denied the right to traverse spaces without being violently interrogated, stopped and frisked, or asked to exit the car.

Mimicking features of Judge Lynch, Zimmerman, as the self-appointed "captain" of the Retreat's neighborhood patrol, performed his sense of belonging by policing The Retreat's "white space" with deadly force. The Retreat's neighborhood watch, which was initiated by Zimmerman, imbued him with the authority to look and judge with impunity. News articles cataloging his numerous emergency and nonemergency phone calls to Sanford police regarding black male intruders testify to Zimmerman's dedication and determination to not let another "coon" get away.[27] Such dedication demonstrates Zimmerman's loyalty and commitment to his imagined the community.

For me, Zimmerman's expressed commitment and procedural actions shed light on Trayvon's description of the "creepy cracker" in pursuit. Zimmerman, who self-identified as "Hispanic," was a light-complexioned man who could easily be mistaken for white on a dark, rainy night like the night of February 26, 2012. Perhaps it was the way Zimmerman performed whiteness—specifically, the way he assumed a supreme right to not only look but profile, surveil, judge, and kill—rather than the condition of being of light skin on a dark night that colored Trayvon's perception of him as the "creepy cracker." If we concede to this possibility, then we might also concede to how it may not have so much been Zimmerman's complexion that directed Trayvon's "misrecognition" of the patrolmen as "white" as perhaps the fact that the self-identified Hispanic was, in a sense, "acting white."

Lewis Gordon extends my sentiment by reading Zimmerman's slaying of Trayvon as a "wage of American membership," suggesting that Zimmerman's mixed-raced status (his mother was of Peruvian descent and his father white) accrued a tax that could be paid only through symbolic labor. Much the way historian Cynthia Skove Nevels explains lynching-to-belong among European immigrants as a means of performing whiteness,[28] Gordon explains Zimmerman's killing of Trayvon as an opportunity to "[r]itualistically . . . affirm his national status through an age-old way of its investment and reinvestment: lynchings and humiliations of blacks, after all, were effective ways not only of keeping black people in line but also of determining which groups are poised for mobility in American membership."[29] In this way Zimmerman's profiling, tracking, stalking, namely, his hunting of Trayvon to his death invoked a legacy of lynching that cast Zimmerman's eradication of Trayvon's black body as the symbolic removal of blackness from the space of white racial belonging that was the Retreat. Trayvon's efforts to evade Zimmerman "the hunter" by running fulfills yet another feature of the lynching narrative in that it indicates not only his sense of impending peril but also his status as always already guilty and thus always already "prey." Their exchange shortly after illustrates, then, a critical difference in what it means to see-in-white as opposed to see-in-black in that both Zimmerman and Trayvon *read* "threat" when they *see* each other, yet whereas Zimmerman's perception of threat is imagined, Trayvon's perception of threat is *real*.

Despite its illegitimacy, Zimmerman's way of seeing Trayvon like Milam's and Bryant's way of seeing Emmett, was legitimated by the state. Milam and Bryant saw Emmett as a threat to white dominance, and the state supported that vision by rendering Emmett nonexistent on account of being unrecognizable. Under this logic, Emmett's rights are not recognized not because the state is complicit in a white supremacist structure, but rather because there is no evidence that a citizen by the name of Emmett Till is dead. Similarly, the verdict rendered during Zimmerman's trial ruled that Zimmerman, who was instructed by dispatch not to follow Trayvon, had a greater right to self-defense and life than the young man he profiled, hunted, and killed. For me, the travesty of Trayvon's death and the acquittal of his killer signify the pervasiveness of a rhetorical and political tradition in which the black body in peril serves as the transcendental signifier of America's white democracy. As Frank Wilderson reminds, the "rhetorical structures and political desires" of white supremacy are "underwritten by a supplemental anti-Blackness" that renders symbolic and material violence against blacks fundamentally "organic to civil society."[30] The state's assistance in Zimmerman's transformation of Trayvon-the-black-citizen into Trayvon-the-lynching-victim, then, demonstrated once again that justice was solely for those deemed just "us." In this sense, we might read Zimmerman's gated community as a microcosm of the nation in that both its physical borders and Zimmerman's citizenly etiquette materially expressed a rhetoric of white citizenship belonging that sought to offer residents of the Retreat an escape from the growing erasure of a white ideal.[31]

Like lynchings in the past, lynchings at the turn of the twenty-first century continue to characterize civic belonging as the ability to kill blacks with impunity.[32] While officers and civilians responsible for the "shooting deaths" of Amadou Diallo (1999), Patrick Dorismond (2000), Trayvon Martin (2012), Mike Brown (2014), Tamir Rice (2014), and Philando Castile (2016) saw time in court, they were neither found guilty nor decertified as policemen.[33] Instead they were promoted or transferred; even those who had been terminated were allowed to continue working as officers in other counties. While the trials that did go forward did more to prosecute victims than perpetrators, the wrongful death suits that followed—which for many was the most readily available means of compelling accountability—simply quantified black life in ways reminiscent of the auction block.[34] The historically successive nature of lynching belies lofty narratives of racial progress to illustrate how antiblack violence shares a relationship of interiority with the making of the nation and maintenance of its people. Contemporary lynchings illustrate the changing same of antiblack racism in America in ways that render moot such colorblind rhetoric as "We are better than this" and "This is not us."[35] Lynching is, to echo Frank Shay, as American as apple pie.[36]

POSTSCRIPT

CAUGHT UP

It was a spectacle—the picnickers drinking and stuffing their faces while I shouted, "I know you see me! I know you see me! I'm not invisible! I know you see me!"

In jail that night I contemplated what I'd just survived. I'd been brutalized, but I was alive. I thought about how my momma would understand me and about how my father would shame me. I could hear him now, "You ain't got no business arguing wit' no cop . . . The only reason you go to jail, Ers, is because you did something wrong." Those words and others reminded me that respectability politics weren't about respect but about surviving the ways America was set up to kill me. According to my father, I was crazy—quite possibly suffering from schizophrenia or some other mental illness that plagued the family. How could I convince a judge that I wasn't crazy if I couldn't even convince my own father?

I thought about the street, about the "Road Closed" signs, and the two white boys walking alongside me but seemingly invisible to Ferrin. It wasn't a mystery how the darkest body in the dark of night could be so readily seen. Crossing the street had been like a game of chicken, and from the instant I was *seen* the mission was to seize me, touch me, twist me, and choke me. . . .

That was May 20, 2014, two days before my father's sixty-third birthday and fourteen months before his death. In the time between then and August 2015, I was fired from my job, forced to take a plea that included nine months' probation and fines, and placed on leave from the university. I spent much of my time orchestrating a defense and making futile attempts to revise this book.

In September 2017 I received a phone call from a Mr. Oliver Mwamba. Oliver recounted a story of attack and terror at the hands of an officer he said I knew.

"His name is Stewart Ferrin, he's the same officer who assaulted you in 2014."

"No, Ferrin's a processor now. He's the one that goes around saying, 'You've been served.'"

"He told me he was a deputy for the sheriff's office," said Oliver.

"What?"

"Yes. I kept asking him why he was doing this and he said, "Because of 'You people.'"

I grew silent then. When Oliver detailed how Ferrin had seized him during a traffic stop, beat him at Taser point, and made him fear for his life and that of his two-year old son, I realized I was wrong. The same man who had attacked me and who I had thought had been censored for his misconduct, had in actuality been only sanctioned; Oliver's attack was the proof.

In 2014 Stewart Ferrin was an employee at the Arizona State University Police Department (ASUPD). Although with them for just under three years, Ferrin had the highest number of complaints, despite the number of veterans in the department. A Notice of Intent to Terminate issued by ASU in January 2015 prompted Ferrin's resignation from ASUPD. From that point on, he worked as a processor, until March 2017, when he was hired as a deputy for the Pinal County Sheriff's Office (PCSO). In December 2017 I received another phone call regarding Stewart Ferrin. The details of Thom Petteruci's story were similar to Oliver's, but with one caveat: Ferrin let Thom go and never reported the stop. Oliver, who is black, is currently battling charges similar to the ones I faced in 2014. Thom, who is white, suffered no such injustice.

In January 2018 I sent a letter to PCSO Sheriff Mark Lamb and all five members of the Pinal County Board of Supervisors regarding Officer Stewart Ferrin's history and his most recent behavior. The letter named official reports that cited Ferrin's "resistance to sound supervisory counseling, coaching, and instruction" and "lack of good judgment and discretion" as chief reasons for his termination. While the PCSO and supervisory board never acknowledged my complaint, the PCSO was forced to address it when the *Phoenix New Times* reported on it in a January 28, 2018, article titled, "The Battle Isn't Over between ASU Professor and Cop Who Arrested Her in 2014." Sensationalized headlines (and viral videos of my attack) aside, the article, despite a subtle undermining of my ethos, legitimated my claims that Officer Stewart Ferrin was unfit to serve and protect.[1] PCSO spokeswoman Navideh Forghani said that Pinal County Sheriff Mark Lamb "stands by Ferrin. . . . We are making sure he stays within our practices . . . We feel very confident he's going to do a really good job." Forghani also stated that Ferrin "has fewer complaints during public contacts compared to the average PCSO deputy.[2] This statement, however, would prove false. On February 1, 2018, the *New Times* followed up with "Bad Math: Pinal Data Worse than Reported on Deputy Who Abused ASU Professor." The article detailed how numbers released by PCSO reflected "a much higher average number of public complaints" for Ferrin "compared to the rest of the department" as officials had previously stated. When asked, Forghani dismissed the discrepancy as an "honest mistake."[3]

While I trust that Sheriff Lamb and the Pinal County Board of Supervisors will do what they can to secure the status quo, it was Forghani's claim of innocence—her little white lie on behalf of the force—that disturbed me the most. Her oversight was no more an innocent error than Pinal County's decision to hire a serial abuser. Such acts, which permit passive-aggressive whiteness to parade as justice, ensure that the culpable are set free to perpetuate misconduct.

The months that followed my attack were populated with black bodies in the street, with the killing of Mike Brown and Ferguson burning, my hometown of Baltimore erupting after the "Freddie Gray verdict," and Charleston mourning. Chants of "Hands up! Don't shoot!" and "I can't breathe" flooded the news, along with protestors who depicted lynching scenes during demonstrations.[4] The year 2014 had been hard, but 2015 proved even harder. That June I watched as Sandra Bland was scapegoated and demonized for standing her ground, lifting her voice, knowing her rights, and fiercely declaring them. I first caught the video while at my father's bedside. Things between us hadn't been the best, and the attack against me only widened the wedge between us. I'd been struggling over what felt like a lack of support from my father—he'd said that what I did was wrong, implied that I was mentally ill, and suggested I had a death wish. So I kept my distance and avoided his calls despite his condition, because arguing with him was not how I wanted to spend our last days together.

I don't know what it's like be a black man in America, to be born in the segregated South of the 1950s, to be a father of black children, to love them, to raise them, to watch them grow. I don't know the fear that attends parenthood, and I don't know what it's like for your children to out the fallacy that you can't protect them. I do know what it's like to be policed by those that love me, to feel my spirit breaking under the tension between being policed and being loved, to understand how the effort to police me the way the system polices all of us is meant to keep me safe.

I did my best to avoid his IV while I leaned in to hug him. His arms were restrained but loose enough so that he could partially hug me back. "I'm sorry, Daddy." He closed his eyes slowly. When he reopened them, shallow pools of water filled the corners. At some point Kanitha had walked in and was now holding me from behind. She leaned in and kissed Daddy.

"I'm sorry," I cried. "I'll do better, I'll work harder to be a lady in the street."

The intubation tube shook as he struggled to shake his head "No."
I made a joke about us not being able to argue properly and watched
his brows rise in agreement. It was sometime after I'd joked about
not going back to jail and watching him roll his eyes that an alert
came on announcing the release of Sandra Bland's arrest video. It
was difficult to see for all my tears but I could hear her perfectly.

"I'm in my car. Why do I have to put out my cigarette?"

We were silent, the three of us. Me, my father, and Kanitha.
Conservative critics, members of the police force, and other talking
heads said that it was Sandra's sass that quickened her death. Others
asserting that contempt wasn't a jailable offense argued that it was
the officer's fragility and the New Jim Crow that killed her, not her
series of reasonable questions. What my father was thinking was all
I wanted to know. But he couldn't talk, he could barely even breathe.

I was reaching for the royal purple bag when my brother walked
in. "Did you see the news?" he asked.

I listened as the ice cubes cracked under the heat of the scotch.
"Yeah," I said. "I saw it."

"I thought it was you . . . she sounded like you."

Four years after my arrest and three years after Sandra's death,
I find myself experiencing more of the same: Walter Scott is dead,
Keith Scott is dead, Korryn Gaines is dead, Philando Castile is dead,
Stephon Clark is dead, and most recently Antwon Rose. Antwon's
killing is particularly troubling for how it echoes my warnings about
Ferrin. Michael Rosfeld, the officer who shot and killed Antwon,
had been previously fired from the University of Pittsburgh police
department for "false arrest, false imprisonment, and malicious
prosecution."[5] The ease with which Ferrin and those like him have
been permitted to terrorize, and the way the system has supported,
encouraged, and rewarded such terror, suggests that the system is
not broken but instead working the way it was intended. It also
evidences that lynching and the discourse substantiating it are
not dead, but rather quite alive. A number of inquiries were sent
to Sheriff Mark Lamb and the Board of Supervisors regarding the

most recent complaints about Ferrin. My hope is that information regarding Ferrin's ongoing history of violent policing will aid Oliver's case and place him one step closer to gaining the justice he so rightly deserves.

NOTES

Author's Note

1. Special thanks to Kishonna Leah Gray-Denson, Stephanie Troutman, Sara Florini, Karma Chavéz, Annie Hill, Jiyeon Kang, Lisa Flores, Heather Switzer, Angela Banks, Victoria Sahani, and Leslie Harris who held and helped me craft this statement.

2. As I write I am reminded of early debate over whether to charge Officer Amber Guyer with *murder* or *manslaughter* in the shooting-death of twenty-six-year-old Botham Shem Jean just this September. I am also recalling how "Stand Your Ground" defenses, like in the killing of Trayvon Martin and most recently Markeis McGlockton, mask *murder* as *manslaughter* in ways that circumvent the relationship between intent and racial bias.

Introduction: A Rhetoric of Civic Belonging

1. Qtd. in George Yancy and Janine Jones, *Pursuing Trayvon Martin: Historical Contexts and Contemporary Manifestations of Racial Dynamics* (Lanham, MD: Lexington Books, 2013), 2–3; Adam Weinstein and MoJo News Team, "The Trayvon Martin Killing, Explained," *Mother Jones*, March 18, 2012, https://www.motherjones .com/politics/2012/03/what-happened-trayvon-martin-explained/; Amy Green, "Zimmerman's Twin Lakes Community Was on Edge before Trayvon Shooting," *Daily Beast*, March 28, 2012, https://www.thedailybeast.com/zimmermans-twin -lakes-community-was-on-edge-before-trayvon-shooting; Ian Tuttle, "The Neighborhood Zimmerman Watched," *National Review*, July 22, 2013, http://www .nationalreview.com/article/354042/neighborhood-zimmerman-watched-ian-tuttle.

2. Zimmerman had contacted the police over forty times about black men burglarizing the neighborhood between August 2004 to the time of the shooting. By February 2012, Zimmerman had secured a gun permit, had purchased a gun, and had been regularly patrolling the neighborhood. For more on Zimmerman's contact with police and preoccupation with policing, see Ian Tuttle, "Neighborhood Zimmerman Watched"; and Chris Francescani, "George Zimmerman: Prelude to a Shooting," *Reuters.com*, April 25, 2012, https://www.reuters.com/article/us-usa -florida-shooting-zimmerman/george-zimmerman-prelude-to-a-shooting -idUSBRE83O18H20120425.

3. Chris Witherspoon, "Harry Belafonte Agrees with Oprah: 'Trayvon Martin Paralleled Emmett Till,'" *Grio*, August 30, 2013, https://thegrio.com/2013/08/30 /harry-belafonte-agrees-with-oprah-trayvon-martin-paralleled-emmett-till/.

4. Chris Witherspoon, "Harry Belafonte Agrees with Oprah: 'Trayvon Martin Paralleled Emmett Till,'" *Grio*, August 30, 2013, https://thegrio.com/2013/08/30 /harry-belafonte-agrees-with-oprah-trayvon-martin-paralleled-emmett-till/

5. Brandon Patterson, "The Cop Who Killed Antwon Rose Violated the Civil Rights of Others, a New Lawsuit Claims," *MotherJones*, July 3, 2018, https://www .motherjones.com/politics/2018/07/lawsuit-east-pittsburgh-cop-who-killed -antwon-rose-violated-civil-rights/.

6. Carrie Heals, "Conservatives Slam Oprah for Trayvon Martin–Emmett Till Comparison," *Grio*, August 8, 2013, https://thegrio.com/2013/08/08/conservatives -slam-oprah-for-trayvon-martin-emmett-till-comparison/; "Oprah's New Shocking Claims!" *FoxNewsInsider*, August 7, 2013, http://insider.foxnews.com/2013/08/07 /oprah-compares-trayvon-martin-emmett-till-says-obama-smart-not-appearing -fox-news.

7. Carrie Heals, "Conservatives Slam Oprah for Trayvon Martin–Emmett Till Comparison," *Grio*, August 8, 2013, https://thegrio.com/2013/08/08/conservatives -slam-oprah-for-trayvon-martin-emmett-till-comparison/.

8. Erica Ritz, "Glenn Beck Takes Apart Oprah's 'Offensive' Trayvon Martin, Emmett Till Comparison during Heartbreaking Segment," *TheBlaze*, August 6, 2013, https:// www.theblaze.com/news/2013/08/06/glenn-beck-calls-oprahs-trayvon-martin -comparison-a-slap-in-the-face-to-memory-of-emmett-till-in-heartbreaking -segment-comparing-the-cases; Carrie Heals, "Conservatives Slam Oprah for Trayvon Martin–Emmett Till Comparison," *Griot*, August 8, 2013, https://thegrio.com/2013/08 /08/conservatives-slam-oprah-for-trayvon-martin-emmett-till-comparison/; "Oprah's New Shocking Claims!" *FoxNewsInsider*, August 7, 2013, http://insider.foxnews.com /2013/08/07/oprah-compares-trayvon-martin-emmett-till-says-obama-smart-not -appearing-fox-news.

9. Glenn Beck, "Glenn Relates Tragic History of Emmett Till in Response to Oprah's Controversial Remarks," *Glennbeck.com*, August 6, 2013, https://www .glennbeck.com/2013/08/06/glenn-relates-tragic-history-of-emmett-till-in -response-to-oprahs-controversial-remarks/.

10. Ashraf Rushdy, *The End of Lynching Discourse* (New Brunswick, NJ: Rutgers University Press, 2012), 96.

11. Rushdy, *End of Lynching Discourse*, 6.

12. Rushdy, *End of Lynching Discourse*, 95.

13. Rushdy, *End of Lynching Discourse*, 103–4.

14. Glenn Beck, "Glenn Relates Tragic History of Emmett Till in Response to Oprah's Controversial Remarks," *Glennbeck.com*, August 6, 2013, https://www .glennbeck.com/2013/08/06/glenn-relates-tragic-history-of-emmett-till-in -response-to-oprahs-controversial-remarks/.

15. Leigh Raiford, "Photography and the Practices of Critical Black Memory," *History and Theory* 48 (December 2009): 119.

16. Raiford, "Photography and the Practices," 119–20.

17. Jesse Carr, "The Lawlessness of Law: Lynching and Anti-lynching in the Contemporary USA," *Settler Colonial Studies* 6, no. 2 (2015): 159.

18. Arthur Raper, *The Tragedy of Lynching* (Mineola, NY: Dover, 2003), 13–16; W. Fitzhugh Brundage, *Lynching in the New South: Georgia and Virginia, 1880–1930* (Urbana: University of Illinois Press, 1993), 30–31.

19. Brundage, *Lynching in the New South*, 30.

20. Raper, *Tragedy of Lynching*, 16.

21. Rallies, demonstrations, and an online petition at Change.org with over 1.5 million signatures called for Zimmerman's prosecution. For more, see Tracy Martin and Sybrina Fulton, "Prosecute the Killer of Our Son, 17-year-old Trayvon Martin," *Change.org*, March 8, 2012, https://www.change.org/p/prosecute-the-killer-of-our -son-17-year-old-trayvon-martin; Madison Gray, "Social Media: The Muscle behind the Trayvon Martin Movement," March 26, 2012, http://newsfeed.time.com/2012/03 /26/social-media-the-muscle-behind-the-trayvon-martin-movement/.

22. Amy Louise Wood, *Lynching and Spectacle: Witnessing Racial Violence in America, 1890–1940* (Chapel Hill: University of North Carolina Press, 2009), 94–99.

23. bell hooks, *Black Looks: Race & Representation* (Boston: South End Press, 1992), 115–33. This is in part what George Yancy means by "walking-in-white." For more, see *Look, a White! Philosophical Essays on Whiteness* (Philadelphia: Temple University Press, 2012), 17–50. We might also recall here how officers culpable in the deaths of Walter Scott and Freddie Gray, respectively, explained their reason for pursuing these men was because of a look each exchanged with the officers who pursued them.

24. Ida B. Wells, "Lynch Law in America," *Arena* 23, no. 1 (1900): 15.

25. Frank Shay, *Judge Lynch: His First Hundred Years* (New York: Biblo and Tannen, 1969), 18–22; James Elbert Cutler, *Lynch-Law: An Investigation into the History of Lynching in the United States* (New York: Longmans, Green), 1905; Ashraf Rushdy, *American Lynching* (New Haven: Yale University Press, 2012), xi–xiii. Charles Lynch is commonly confused with his brother, John Lynch, who founded the town of Lynchburg, Virginia.

26. Anderson Benedict, *Imagined Communities* (New York: Verso, 1991); Michael Warner, *Publics and Counterpublics* (New York: Zone Books, 2005); Gregory Clark, *Rhetorical Landscapes* (Columbia: University of South Carolina Press, 2004).

27. "The Dogwood Tree," lynching postcard poem, juxtaposes an image of the 1908 lynching of five black men in Sabine County, Texas, with a poem called "The Dogwood Tree" that celebrates lynching as a performance of white supremacy. The image was published by Harkrider Drug Co., Center, Texas.

28. After pleading guilty, the accused was not punished until he shouted, "Liberty forever!" The names listed in the chorus are those of Captain Robert "Bob" Adams, Jr., Colonel James Callaway, and William Preston, all associated justices of Colonel Charles Lynch's court. Shay, *Judge Lynch*, 23.

29. Rushdy, *American Lynching*, xiii, 2, 22–27.

30. Shay, *Judge Lynch*, 18–19.

31. Shay, *Judge Lynch*, 18–26, 116. Also see Walter White, *Rope and Faggot: A Biography of Judge Lynch* (Notre Dame, IN: University of Notre Dame Press, 2001), 82–84; Christopher Waldrep, *African Americans Confront Lynching: Strategies of Resistance from the Civil War to the Civil Rights Era* (Lanham, MD: Rowman and Littlefield, 2008), 2.

32. Christopher Waldrep. *The Many Faces of Judge Lynch* (Notre Dame: University of Notre Dame Press, 2001), 16–17.

33. Jefferson to Charles Lynch, August 1, 1780, *Papers of Thomas Jefferson*, 3:523.

34. Shay, *Judge Lynch*, 23.

35. Shay, *Judge Lynch*, 24–26.

36. Shay, *Judge Lynch*, 25.

37. Rushdy, *American Lynching*, 57; Jacqueline Goldsby, *A Spectacular Secret: Lynching in American Life and Literature* (Chicago: University of Chicago Press, 2006), 16–17.

38. Alison Piepmier, *Out in Public: Configurations of Women's Bodies in Nineteenth-Century America* (Chapel Hill: University of North Carolina Press, 2004), 137.

39. Charles Mills, *The Racial Contract* (Ithaca: Cornell University Press, 1997), 3, 12–15.

40. Mills, *Racial Contract*, 12–14.

41. Mills, *Racial Contract*, 25.

42. David Roediger, *Wages of Whiteness: Race and the Making of American Working Class*. Revised Edition (Verso: New York, 2007), 57.

43. Mills, *Racial Contract*, 3.

44. Mills, *Racial Contract*, 14.

45. Mills, *Racial Contract*, 56.

46. Jacqueline Jones Royster, ed., *Southern Horrors and Other Writings: The Anti-lynching Campaign of Ida B. Wells, 1892–1900* (Boston: Bedford/St. Martin's Press, 1997), 29–30.

47. Wells, "Lynch Law in America," 15–24.

48. Clark, *Rhetorical Landscapes*, 15.

49. Danielle Allen, *Talking to Strangers: Anxieties of Citizenship since "Brown v. Board of Education"* (Chicago: University of Chicago Press, 2006), 1–8; Stephen Berrey, *The Jim Crow Routine: Everyday Performances of Race, Civil Rights, and Segregation in Mississippi* (Chapel Hill: University of North Carolina Press, 2005), 34–42.

50. Goldsby, *Spectacular Secret*, 17.

51. Jennie Lightweis-Goff, *Blood at the Root: Lynching as American Cultural Nucleus* (Albany: SUNY Press, 2011), 4–5.

52. Taney Roger, *The Dred Scott Decision: Opinion of Chief Justice Taney* (New York: Van Evrie, Horton, 1860), https://www.loc.gov/resource/llst.022/?sp=18.

53. Cynthia Skove Nevels, *Lynching to Belong: Claiming Whiteness through Racial Violence* (College Station: Texas A&M University Press, 2007).

54. Dora Apel, *Imagery of Lynching: Black Men, White Women, and the Mob* (New Brunswick: Rutgers University Press, 2004), 27.

55. Sandy Alexandre, *Properties of Violence: Claims to Ownership in Representations of Lynching* (Jackson: University Press of Mississippi, 2012), 87.

56. Wood, Lynching and Spectacle, 11.

57. Charles Griswold and Stephen Griswold. "The Vietnam Veterans Memorial and the Washington Mall: Philosophical Thoughts on Political Iconography," *Critical Inquiry* 12, no. 4 (1986): 689.

58. Wells, *Lynch Law in America*; Rushdy, *American Lynching*.

59. Amy Louise Wood and Susan Donaldson, "Lynching's Legacy in American Culture," *Mississippi Quarterly* 61, no. 1/2 (2008):13; Ashraf Rushdy, *The End of American Lynching* (New Brunswick: Rutgers University Press, 2012), 16.

60. Rushdy, *End of American Lynching*, 95–96.

61. Rushdy, *End of American Lynching*, 103–4 (emphasis added).

62. "Statement to the Media by the United Nations' Working Group of Experts on People of African Descent, on the inclusion of Its Official Visit to USA, 19–29 January 2016," *United Nations Human Rights Office of the High Commissioner.* January 29, 2016, http://ohchr.org/EN/NewsEvents/Pages/DisplayNews.aspx ?NewsID=17000&LangID=E.

63. Bryan Stevenson, *Just Mercy: A Story of Justice and Redemption* (New York: Spiegel & Grau, 2015).

64. *Lynching in America: Confronting the Legacy of Racial Terror*, 3rd ed., the Equal Justice Initiative, https://lynchinginamerica.eji.org/report/.

65. Dave Zirin, "Why I Called the Murder of Richard Collins III a 'Lynching,'" *Nation*, May 25, 2017, https://www.thenation.com/article/called-murder-richard -collins-iii-lynching/.

66. Angela Helm, "Parents of Teen Accused of Nearly Hanging 8-Year-Old Say It Was an 'Accident' (and They Have Black Family, Too)," *Root*, September 25, 2017,

https://www.theroot.com/parents-of-teen-accused-of-nearly-hanging-8-year-old
-sa-1818732787.

67. Jamie Seaton, "New Hampshire Hanging: Parents of Accused Teen Say It Was
an Accident Not a Lynching," *Newsweek*, September 23, 2017, http://www.newsweek
.com/hanging-boy-biracial-8-years-old-black-white-new-hampshire-lynching
-claremont-664415.

68. Helm, "Parents of Teen Accused."

69. Eduardo Bonilla-Silva, *Racism without Racists: Color-Blind Racism and
the Persistence of Racial Inequality in America*, 3rd ed. (Lanham, MD: Rowman &
Littlefield, 2009), 53–74.

70. Quincy and Ayanna's mother reported the psychological impact of the
incident: Quincy suffers from night terrors, and Ayanna, who was reportedly being
taunted about the incident, suffered a loss of appetite and also struggled to sleep.

71. Sindiso Minsi Weeks and Dan Weeks, "Call a Lynching by Its Name," *New
York Times*, September 26, 2017, https://kristof.blogs.nytimes.com/2017/09/26/call
-a-lynching-by-its-name/.

72. Zirin, "Why I Called."

73. Yancy, *Look, a White!*, 17–50.

74. Safia Ali, "Fired Officer Who Shot Tamir Rice Could Be Back at Another
Department," *NBC News*, June 2, 2017, https://www.nbcnews.com/news/us-news
/fired-officer-who-shot-tamir-rice-could-be-back-another-n766921.

75. The wrongful death settlements of black men from 1999 to 2016 ranged
between 1.5 million and 6 million dollars. For more on wrongful death settlements of unarmed black men, see Ryllie Danylko, "Tamir Rice Settlement: How
Cleveland's $6 Million Payout Compares with Similar Cases in US," *Cleveland.com*,
April 25, 2016, http://www.cleveland.com/metro/index.ssf/2016/04/how_the_tamir
_rice_settlement.html; Jim Salter, "Ferguson Attorney: Brown Family Wrongful
Death Settlement Is $1.5 Million," *Chicago Tribune*, June 24, 2017, http://www
.chicagotribune.com/news/nationworld/ct-ferguson-brown-family-settlement
-20170623-story.html; Amy Forliti, "Philando Castile Family Reaches $3M
Settlement in Death, *Chicago Tribune*, June 26, 2017, http://www.chicagotribune.
com/news/nationworld/ct-philando-castile-death-settlement-20170626-story.html;
William Glaberson, "City Settles Suit in Guard's Death by Police Bullet," *New York
Times*, March 13, 2003, http://www.nytimes.com/2003/03/13/nyregion/city-settles
-suit-in-guard-s-death-by-police-bullet.html.

76. Frank B. Wilderson, "The Prison Slave as Hegemony's (Silent) Scandal,"
Social Justice 30, no. 2 (2003), 7.

Chapter One. Constituting the "Citizen Race"

1. Patricia Williams, *Alchemy of Race & Rights* (Cambridge: Harvard
University Press, 1991), 50.

2. Kenneth Burke, *A Grammar of Motives* (Berkeley: University of California Press, 1969), 19–22, 59.

3. Jeremy Engels, *Enemyship: Democracy and Counter-Revolution in the Early Republic* (East Lansing: Michigan State University Press, 2010), 13–22; Frank Wilderson, "The Prison Slave as Hegemony's (Silent) Scandal," *Social Justice* 30, no. 2 (2003).

4. Lisa A. Flores, "Constructing Rhetorical Borders: Peons, Illegal Aliens, and Competing Narratives of Immigration," *Critical Studies in Media Communication* 20, no. 4 (December 2003): 362–87; Robert DeChaine, ed., *Border Rhetorics: Citizenship and Identity on the US–Mexico Frontier* (Tuscaloosa: University of Alabama Press, 2012); Kent Ono and John Sloop, *Shifting Borders: Rhetoric, Immigration, and California's Proposition 187* (Philadelphia: Temple University Press, 2008).

5. Thomas Jefferson, Declaration of Independence, 1776.

6. By 1780 antislavery sentiment had grown. Following Pennsylvania's 1780 Act of Gradual Abolition, every state in New England except Massachusetts implemented gradual abolition. Slavery was instantly abolished in 1783 after the Massachusetts Supreme Court ruled the institution illegal. Accompanying legislative reforms was a growing antislavery movement. Thus, despite later restrictions on assemblage, migration, employment, and initiatives to relocate free blacks to Africa, Northerners generally held to their indictment of slavery.

7. Winthrop Jordan, *White over Black: American Attitudes toward the Negro, 1550–1812* (Chapel Hill: University of North Caroline Press, 1968), 322; Thomas West, *Vindicating the Founders* (Lanham, MD: Rowman and Littlefield, 2005), 15; Joel Olson, *Abolition of White Democracy* (Minneapolis: University of Minnesota Press, 2004).

8. U.S. Constitution, Article 1, Section 2.

9. Naturalization Act of 1790, 1 Stat. 103–4 (emphasis added).

10. Rogers Smith, *Civic Ideals: Conflicting Visions of Citizenship in U.S. History* (New Haven: Yale University Press, 1997), 119.

11. Smith, *Civic Ideals*, 215; 105–6.

12. Smith, *Civic Ideals*, 105–6.

13. John Hope Franklin, *The Militant South, 1800–1861* (Urbana: University of Illinois Press, 1967), 76 (uppercase original)

14. Solomon Northup, *12 Years a Slave* (Bedford, MA: Applewood Books, 1853); Smith, *Civic Ideals*, 119, 253.

15. Roger Taney, *The Dred Scott Decision: Opinion of Chief Justice Taney* (New York: Van Evrie, Horton, 1860), https://www.loc.gov/resource/llst.022/?sp=18.

16. Taney, *Dred Scott Decision* (emphasis added).

17. Mark Weiner, *Black Trails: Citizenship from the Beginnings of Slavery to the End of Caste* (New York: Alfred Knopf, 2004), 94.

18. Some of the first explicitly raced-based laws were drafted during the seventeenth century in Virginia, the most prominent and influential territory among the

colonies. Over 40 percent of American slaves resided in Virginia. The black codes
of the seventeenth century were implemented in efforts to deter political and sexual liaisons among African and European indentured servants. For more on raced-
based laws before the nineteenth century, see Edmund Morgan, *American Slavery,
American Freedom: The Ordeal of Colonial Virginia* (New York: W. W. Norton, 1975),
335–37. Also see Rushdy, *American Lynching*, 59–60.

   19. Eric Foner, *Reconstruction: America's Unfinished Revolution, 1863–1877*
(Chicago: University of Chicago Press, 2005), 200; John Hope Franklin,
Reconstruction after the Civil War (Chicago: University of Chicago Press, 1994), 48.
For more details, see Wilson, *Black Codes of 1866*, 96–115.

   20. Franklin, *Reconstruction after the Civil War*, 48–51; Foner, *Reconstruction*,
199–200; Theodore Wilson, *Black Codes of the South* (Tuscaloosa: University of
Alabama Press, 1965), 99.

   21. Foner, *Reconstruction*, 199–200.

   22. Wilson, *Black Codes*, 39; Foner, *Reconstruction*, 201.

   23. Foner, *Reconstruction*, 203.

   24. Foner, *Reconstruction*, 209.

   25. Franklin, *Reconstruction after the Civil War*.

   26. The Freemen's Bureau bill, which was a response to the black codes of 1866,
sought to extend the bureau's jurisdictional power so as to protect freemen from
social, political, and legal abuses. After Johnson's veto of the bureau's bill, Congress
submitted the Civil Rights bill. The Civil Rights Act was the second attempt by
Congress to secure black freedom and enfranchisement. It was considered the first
Reconstruction act and later became the Fourteenth Amendment. Despite his protest, however, Johnson's attempts to thwart congressional Reconstruction failed. His
March 27 veto of the Civil Rights bill was overridden by the Senate on April 6, and
the House three days later.

   27. Smith, 291–94; Todd McDorman, "History, Collective Memory, and the
Supreme Court: Debating 'the People' through the Dred Scott Controversy,"
Southern Communication Journal 71, no. 3 (2006): 213–34.

   28. *Congressional Globe*, 39th Congress, 1st sess., 880. Also see T. A. Hendricks,
speech of Hon. T. A. Hendricks, of Indiana: In the Senate of the United States,
February 16, 1866.

   29. *Congressional Globe*, 39th Congress, 1st sess., 217.

   30. Franklin, *Reconstruction after the Civil War*, 74.

   31. "Negro Rule" was a common euphemism that implied the "radical" nature
of congressional Reconstruction. The phrase was standard in the discourse debas-
ing blacks and black citizenship. Johnson, himself a poor North Carolinian of
yeomanry roots, believed that the planter elite and laboring blacks conspired to
thwart the interests of white workers. Pulling from his prejudice against both
groups, he contended that granting blacks the vote would only strengthen this

dynamic by placing political power in the hands of former slaves who, following the interest and direction of past masters, would continue to deprive poor whites of fair participation in labor. For more on "Negrò Rule," see Franklin, *Reconstruction,* 132–33; Helen Edmonds, *The Negro and Fusion Politics in North Carolina, 1894–1901* (Chapel Hill: University of North Carolina Press, 2003); John Lynch, *Reminiscences of an Active Life: The Autobiography of John Roy Lynch* (Jackson: University Press of Mississippi, 2008), 131–37. For more on Johnson and yeomanry roots, see Foner, *Reconstruction,* 180–81; Franklin, *Reconstruction,* 70–74; W. Fitzhugh Brundage, *Lynching in the New South: Georgia and Virginia, 1880–1930* (Champaign: University of Illinois Press, 1993), 23–27.

32. "The Vampire That Hovers over North Carolina," *News and Observer* (Raleigh, NC), September 27, 1898, *The 1898 Election in North Carolina, UNC Libraries,* accessed June 3, 2016, http://exhibits.lib.unc.edu/exhibits/show/1898/item /2215; "Remember!" cartoon, *News and Observer* (Raleigh, NC), November 3, 1898, *The 1898 Election in North Carolina, UNC Libraries,* accessed June 3, 2016, http:// exhibits.lib.unc.edu/exhibits/show/1898/item/2244; "Don't Be Tempted by the Devil," *News and Observer* (Raleigh, NC), October 26, 1898, *The 1898 Election in North Carolina, UNC Libraries,* accessed June 3, 2016, http://exhibits.lib.unc.edu /exhibits/show/1898/item/2238.

33. *Congressional Globe,* 39th Congress, 2nd Session 1 (1867). For more on Johnson's incendiary rhetoric and antiblack citizenship stance, see Foner, *Reconstruction,* 180.

34. This average of data provided by Franklin, *Reconstruction,* 101–2. Also see "Negro Rule," *Troy (New York) Weekly Times,* August 31, 1867. While blacks constituted a majority in these state legislatures, they failed to grasp the governorship and other significant local offices. For more on the duration of black legislative majority, see Franklin, *Reconstruction,* 85–94, 132–37; and Foner, *Reconstruction,* 351–58.

35. Although Georgia was readmitted to the Union in 1868, it was quickly expelled a year later, because legislators refused to ratify the Fifteenth Amendment. Once they ratified it, in 1870, the state was readmitted. For more, see Franklin, *Reconstruction,* 54–68.

36. Franklin, *Reconstruction,* 130–32.

37. Orlando Patterson, *Rituals of Blood: Consequences of Slavery in Two American Centuries* (Washington, DC: Civitas/Counterpoint, 1998), 174–76. In *Lynching in the New South,* Brundage estimates a total 3,220 blacks were lynched between 1880 and 1930. For more, see Brundage, *Lynching in the New South,* 8.

38. For more on economic factors contributing to lynching, see Oliver Cox, "Lynching and the Status Quo," *Journal of Negro Education* 14, no. 4 (1945): 576–88; Foner, *Reconstruction,* 119–76; Brundage, *Lynching in the New South,* 23–28.

39. Brundage, *Lynching in the New South,* 55.

40. Brundage, *Lynching in the New South,* 57.

41. Brundage, *Lynching in the New South*, 55–56.

42. Patterson, *Rituals of Blood*, "Table 2.1 Alleged Reasons for Lynching, 1882–1968," 175.

43. Brundage, *Lynching in the New South*, Appendix A, Table 3, "Lynchings of Blacks, 1880–1930," 263.

44. There are conflicting accounts of the Memphis lynching. Ida B. Wells, friend and godmother to the daughter of Thomas Moss, was the first to relay an account. In her autobiography, *Crusade for Justice*, Wells recalls that the men at the Curve beat the white men. However, in Patricia A. Schechter's research on the incident, she suggests that there was no fight, but rather a verbal confrontation. And while Wells recalls that the black men received nominal fines for their actions, Schechter reports that a warrant for the arrest of Thomas Moss on charges of assault and battery was issued. For more, see Patricia Ann Schechter, *Ida B. Wells-Barnett and American Reform, 1880–1930* (Chapel Hill: University of North Carolina Press, 2001), 77; Alfreda Duster, *Crusade for Justice: The Autobiography of Ida B. Wells* (Chicago: University of Chicago Press, 1972), 47–52; Jacqueline Jones Royster, ed., *Southern Horrors and Other Writings: The Anti-lynching Campaign of Ida B. Wells, 1892–1900* (Boston: Bedford/St. Martin's Press, 1997), 64–65.

45. Duster, *Crusade for Justice*, 47–52; Schechter, *Ida B. Wells-Barnett*, 75–78.

46. Brundage, *Lynching in the South*, 24.

47. Alexandre, *Properties of Violence*, 87. Also see Royster, *Southern Horrors*, 58–59; Hazel Carby, *Reconstructing Womanhood: The Emergence of the Afro-American Woman Novelist* (Oxford: Oxford University Press, 1989), 115; Patricia Hill Collins, *Black Feminist Thought: Knowledge, Consciousness, and the Politics of Empowerment* (New York: Routledge, 1999).

48. Arthur Raper, *The Tragedy of Lynching* (Mineola, NY: Dover, 2003), 144.

49. Raper, *Tragedy of Lynching*, 147.

50. Qtd. from the Macon *Telegraph*, in Raper, *Tragedy of Lynching*, 147–48 (emphasis added).

51. Rushdy, *American Lynching*, 37. Also see Amy Louise Wood, *Lynching and Spectacle: Witnessing Racial Violence in America, 1890–1940* (Chapel Hill: University of North Carolina Press, 2009), 98–100; Alexandre, *Properties*, 83–87.

52. Qtd. in Royster, *Southern Horrors*, 52–59.

53. Qtd. in Royster, *Southern Horrors*, 52, 78.

54. James R. Browning. "Anti-Miscegenation Laws in the United States," *Duke Bar Journal* 1, no. 1 (1951): 26–41; see Milton Barron, *People Who Intermarry: Intermarriage in a New England Industry Community* (Syracuse: Syracuse University Press, 1946), 117–18.

55. For more on economic factors contributing to lynching, see Oliver Cox, "Lynching and the Status Quo," *Journal of Negro Education* 14, no. 4 (1945): 576–88; Foner, *Reconstruction*, 119–76; Brundage, *Lynching in the New South*, 23–28.

56. Robyn Wiegman, "The Anatomy of a Lynching," *Journal of the History of Sexuality*. 3, no. 3, special issue "African American Culture and Sexuality" (January 1993): 455.

57. Gregory Clark, *Rhetorical Landscapes* (Columbia: University of South Carolina Press, 2004), 14.

58. For more on lynching and space, see Sheryl Ifill, *On the Courthouse Lawn: Confronting the Legacy of Lynching in the Twenty-First Century* (Boston: Beacon Press, 2007).

59. Leigh Raiford, *Imprisoned in a Luminous Glare: Photography and the African American Freedom Struggle* (Chapel Hill: University of North Carolina Press, 2013), 39.

60. Ralph Ginzburg, *100 Years of Lynching* (Baltimore: Black Classic Press, 1996), 10, 12, 22, 50, 34; Susan Jean, "'Warranted' Lynchings: Narratives of Mob Violence in White Southern Newspapers, 1880–1940," *American Nineteenth Century History* 6, no. 3 (2005): 351–72; Dora Apel, *Imagery of Lynching: Black Men, White Women, and the Mob* (New Brunswick: Rutgers University Press, 2004), 201; Amy Louise Wood, "Lynching Photography and the Visual Reproduction of White Supremacy," *American Nineteenth Century History* 6, no. 3 (2005): 374.

61. James Madison, *A Lynching in the Heartland* (New York: Palgrave Macmillan, 2001); Philip Dray, *At the Hands of Persons Unknown* (New York: Random House, 2002); Cynthia Carr, *Our Town: A Heartland Lynching, a Haunted Town, and the Hidden History of White America* (New York: Crown, 2006).

62. A common refrain used in autopsy reports and court documents that distinguished protected perpetrators from prosecution and contributed to lynching terror. For more, see Dray, *At the Hands of Persons Unknown*, ix–xi.

63. Clark, *Rhetorical Landscapes*.

Chapter Two. A Lesson in Civics

1. Ralph Ellison, *Invisible Man* (New York: Random House, 1995), 39.

2. Jerry Bryant, *Victims and Heroes: Racial Violence in the African American Novel* (Amherst: University of Massachusetts Press, 1997), 76.

3. Aristotle, *On Rhetoric: A Theory of Civic Discourse*, trans. George Kennedy (Oxford: Oxford University Press, 2006); Cynthia Sheard, "The Public Value of Epideictic Rhetoric," *College English* 58, no. 7 (1996): 765–94.

4. Chaim Perelman and Lucie Olbrechts-Tyteca, *The New Rhetoric: A Treatise on Argumentation* (Notre Dame, IN: University of Notre Dame Press, 1971); Christine Oravec, "'Observation' in Aristotle's Theory of Epideictic Rhetoric," *Philosophy and Rhetoric* 9 (1976): 162–74; Kathleen Hall Jamieson and Karlyn Kohrs Campbell, "Rhetorical Hybrids: Fusions of Generic Elements," *Quarterly Journal of*

Speech 68, no. 2 (1982): 146–57; Gregory Clark, *Rhetorical Landscapes* (Columbia: University of South Carolina Press, 2004), 19–23.

5. Amy Louise Wood, *Lynching and Spectacle: Witnessing Racial Violence in America, 1890–1940* (Chapel Hill: University of North Carolina Press, 2009); Robert Hariman and John Louis Lucaites, *No Caption Needed: Iconic Photographs, Public Culture, and Liberal Democracy* (Chicago: University of Chicago Press, 2011), 9.

6. John C. Adams, "Epideictic and Its Cultural Reception: In Memory of the Firefighters," in *Rhetorics of Display*, ed. Lawrence J. Prelli (Columbia: University of South Carolina Press, 2006), 297.

7. Perleman and Olbrechts-Tyteca, *New Rhetoric*, 52.

8. Adams, "Epideictic and Its Cultural Reception," 296.

9. Margaret LaWare, "Encountering Visions of Aztlán: Arguments for Ethnic Pride, Community Activism and Cultural Revitalization in Chicano Murals," in *Visual Rhetoric: A Reader in Communication and American Culture*, ed. Lester Olson, Cara Finnegan, and Diane Hope (Los Angeles: SAGE, 2008), 230. Following Lawrence Rosenfield's work on epideictic rhetoric, LaWare contends that the visual image functions didactically by presenting "particular claims about the community it addresses" and "about how it should view itself." Also see Olson et al., *Visual Rhetoric*; Charles Hill and Marguerite Helmers, *Defining Visual Rhetorics* (New York: Routledge, 2004); Hariman and Lucaites, *No Caption Needed.*

10. Hariman and Lucaites, *No Caption Needed*, 27, 12; Christa Olson, *Constitutive Visions: Indigeneity and Commonplaces of National Identity in Republican Ecuador* (University Park: Penn State University Press, 2013), 11–14.

11. Hariman and Lucaites, *No Caption Needed*, 9; Danielle Allen, *Talking to Strangers: Anxieties of Citizenship since "Brown v. Board of Education"* (Chicago: University of Chicago Press, 2004), 5–6.

12. Charles Mills, *The Racial Contract* (Ithaca: Cornell University Press, 1997); Joel Olson, *Abolition of White Democracy* (Minneapolis: University of Minnesota Press, 2004).

13. Michael Shapiro, *The Politics of Representation: Writing Practices in Biography, Photography, and Policy Analysis* (Madison: University of Wisconsin Press, 1988), 124–93, 141; Alan Trachtenberg, *Reading American Photographs: Images as History, Matthew Brady to Walker Evans* (New York: Noonday Press, 1989); Wood, *Lynching and Spectacle*, 84–94.

14. Hariman and Lucaites, *No Caption Needed*, 2–12. Also see Shapiro, *The Politics of Representation*; Suren Lalvani, *Photography, Vision, and the Production of Modern Bodies* (1995); Victor Burgin, *In/Different Spaces: Place and Memory in Visual Culture* (Albany: State University of New York Press, 1996); Wood, *Lynching and Spectacle.*

15. Wood, *Lynching and Spectacle*, 86–98; Leigh Raiford, "Lynching, Visuality, and the Un/Making of Blackness," *NKA: Journal of Contemporary African Art* 20 (2006): 26.

16. Amy Louise Wood, "Lynching Photography and the Visual Reproduction of White Supremacy," *American Nineteenth Century History* 6, no. 3 (2005): 375.

17. Wood, *Lynching and Spectacle*, 86–99.

18. Wood, "Lynching Photography," 376.

19. Ralph Ginzburg, *100 Years of Lynching* (Baltimore: Black Classic Press, 1996), 9–12, 22, 34, 50.

20. By facilitating the circulation of lynching postcards, the US postal system demonstrated its adherence to the politics sustaining white supremacy and its role as an instrument of white democracy. Changing sentiment, however, resulted in the 1908 passage of a law prohibiting the circulation of "matter of a character tending to incite arson, murder, and assassination" (Qtd. in Ashraf Rushdy, *The End of American Lynching* [New Brunswick: Rutgers University Press, 2012], 69).

21. Hill and Helmers, *Defining Visual Rhetorics*, 1.

22. Wood, *Lynching and Spectacle*, 93; Thérèse Smith, "Lyrical Protest: Music in the History of African American Culture," in *Human Bondage in the Cultural Contact Zone: Transdisciplinary Perspectives on Slavery and Its Discourses*, ed. Raphael Hormann and Gesa Mackenthun (Münster: Waxmann Verlag, 2010), 264.

23. For more on the use of lynching photographs in the dissemination of racist ideology, see Dora Apel and Shawn Michelle Smith, *Lynching Photographs, Defining Moments in American Photography* (Berkeley: University of California Press, 2008). For lynching photographs and their role in the construction of whiteness, see Shawn Michelle Smith, *Photography on the Color Line: W. E. B. Du Bois, Race, and Visual Culture* (Durham: Duke University Press, 2004), 118–46; Dora Apel and Shawn Michelle Smith, *Lynching Photographs* (Berkeley: University of California Press, 2008), 14–25, 46; Wood, *Lynching and Spectacle*, 9; James Allen, *Without Sanctuary: Lynching Photography in America* (San Francisco: Twin Palms, 2000), 26; Raiford, "Lynching, Visuality, and the Un/Making of Blackness," 26.

24. Smith, *Photography on the Color Line*, 122.

25. Scholars of lynching contend that lynching photographs invite viewers to either assume or negate the subject positions of those depicted. For more on lynching and the constitutive power of looking, see Apel and Smith, *Lynching Photographs*, 14–15; Wood, *Spectacle of Lynching*, 3–11.

26. Jacqueline Jones Royster, ed., *Southern Horrors and Other Writings: The Anti-lynching Campaign of Ida B. Wells, 1892–1900* (Boston: Bedford/St. Martin's Press, 1997), 106–17.

27. Royster, *Southern Horrors*, 104.

28. Royster, *Southern Horrors*, 116.

29. Royster, *Southern Horrors*, 116; Rushdy, *End of American Lynching*, 140.

30. Rushdy, *End of American Lynching*, 68.

31. Qtd. in Alfreda Duster, *Crusade for Justice: The Autobiography of Ida B. Wells* (Chicago: University of Chicago Press, 1972), 52.

32. Duster, *Crusade for Justice*, 47–52.

33. Royster, *Southern Horrors*, 28–29; Wells-Barnett, "Lynch Law," in *The Reason Why the Colored American Is Not in the World's Columbian Exposition: The Afro-American's Contribution to Columbian Literature*, ed. Robert Rydell (Chicago: University of Illinois Press, 1893), 29.

34. Eric Foner, *Reconstruction: America's Unfinished Revolution, 1863–1877* (Chicago: Chicago University Press, 2005), 209.

35. "The Lynching in Lee County, Ga.," *Crisis*, April 1916, 302.

36. "Lynching in Lee County, Ga.," 302.

37. "Lynching in Lee County, Ga.," 304 (emphasis added).

38. William Jordan, *Black Newspapers & America's War for Democracy, 1914–1920* (Chapel Hill: University of North Carolina Press, 2001), 41–43.

39. James Weldon Johnson, "Is This Civilization?" *New York Age*, January 21, 1915, p. 4.

40. For more on critiques of mainstream white newspapers during World War II, see Jordan, *Black Newspapers*; Ida B. Wells-Barnett, *The Red Record: Tabulated Statistics and Alleged Causes of Lynching in the United States* (Project Gutenberg Ebook), 31–56; Royster, *Southern Horrors*, 106–17.

41. "To the Presidential Nominee," *Chicago Defender*, June 20, 1916.

42. The city of Eau Gallie, Florida, has since been absorbed by the city of Melbourne. It currently appears as a neighborhood located in the northern district of Melbourne, Florida. For more, see Amy Bailey, *Lynched: The Victims of Southern Mob Violence* (Chapel Hill: University of North Carolina Press, 2015), 36–39; Ben Brotemarkle, "Brevard's Last Lynching Took Place in 1926," *Florida Frontiers*, August 30, 2016, https://www.floridatoday.com/story/news/2016/08/29/florida-frontiers-lynching-james-clark/89531344/.

43. Qtd. in Brotemarkle, "Brevard's Last Lynching."

44. Leigh Raiford, "Photography and the Practices of Critical Black Memory," *History and Theory* 48 (December 2009): 112–29.

45. "My Country, 'Tis of Thee, Sweet Land of Liberty—," *Crisis* 42, no. 2 (1935): 57.

46. Davis Houck and Matthew Grindy, *Emmett Till and the Mississippi Press* (Jackson: University Press of Mississippi, 2010), 16. Two months following *Brown*, the Citizens' Council boasted headquarters in Mississippi, Alabama, and Arkansas, and more than 25,000 members. For more on the Citizens' Council, see Alfred Maund, "Grass-Roots Racism: White Council at Work," *Nation* 4 (1955): 70–72; Neil McMillen, *The Citizens' Council: Organized Resistance to the Second Reconstruction, 1954–1964* (Champaign: University of Illinois Press, 1971).

47. Davis Houck, "Killing Emmett," *Rhetoric & Public Affairs* 8, no. 2 (2005): 230–39; Houck and Grindy, *Emmett Till*, 16.

48. Stephen Whitfield, *A Death in the Delta: The Story of Emmett Till* (Baltimore: Johns Hopkins University Press, 1988), 10.

49. While Carolyn Bryant testified to being assaulted, she later admitted that it was not true. For more, see Timothy Tyson, *The Blood of Emmett Till* (New York: Simon and Schuster, 2017).

50. More details regarding motivations for such haste, see Davis and Grindy, *Emmett Till*, 22.

51. Mamie Till-Mobley and Christopher Benson, *Death of Innocence: The Story of a Hate Crime That Changed America* (New York: Random House, 2003), 139.

52. Christopher Metress, ed., *The Lynching of Emmett Till: A Documentary Narrative* (Charlottesville: University of Virginia Press, 2002), 227.

53. Courtney Baker, "Emmett Till, Justice, and the Task of Recognition," *Journal of American Culture* 29, no. 2 (2006): 115.

54. The estimated number of people who visited Till's body during the course of its three-day lying-in-state varies among newspapers and historical, as well as critical, accounts of the event. See Devery Anderson, *Emmett Till: The Murder That Shocked the World and Propelled the Civil Rights Movement* (Jackson: University Press of Mississippi, 2015), 56.

55. Anderson, *Emmett Till*, 45–47.

56. Anderson, *Emmett Till*, 138. Houck and Grindy's analysis of various documents and local press coverage of the Till trial contradicts Strider's testimony. As they demonstrate, Strider had confirmed as early as September 1 not only that the body was Emmett's but also that the body had been in the river for only "about two days" (161). For more, see Houck and Grindy, *Emmett Till*, 21–22, 34–39; Anderson, *Emmett Till*, 161.

57. Anderson, *Emmett Till*, 139–41.

58. Till-Mobley and Benson, *Death of Innocence*, 103–4; Valerie Smith, "Emmett Till's Ring," *WSQ: Women's Studies Quarterly* 36, no. 1–2 (2008): 151; Houck and Grindy, *Emmett Till*, 34.

59. Till-Mobley and Benson, *Death of Innocence*, 178–80; Metress, *Lynching of Emmett Till*, 226; Christine Harold and Kevin Michael DeLuca, "Behold the Corpse: Violent Images and the Case of Emmett Till," *Rhetoric & Public Affairs* 8, no. 2 (2005): 264.

60. William Bradford Huie, "The Shocking Story of Approved Killing in Mississippi," in *A History in Documents: Lynching in America*, ed. Christopher Waldrep (New York: New York University Press, 2006), 255–57 (emphasis added).

61. Truider Harris, *Exorcising Blackness: Historical and Literary Lynching and Burning Rituals* (Bloomington: Indiana University Press, 1984), 70.

62. Raiford, "Photography and the Practices"; Leigh Raiford, *Imprisoned in a Luminous Glare: Photography and the African American Freedom Struggle* (Chapel Hill: University of North Carolina Press, 2011), 16–17, 62–64.

63. Wood, Lynching and Spectacle, 4; Christa Olson, *Constitutive Visions: Indigeneity and Commonplaces of National Identity in Republican Ecuador* (University Park: Penn State University Press, 2013), 1–13.

64. Metress, *Lynching of Emmett Till*, 263.

65. Anne Moody, *Coming of Age in Mississippi* (New York: Dial Press, 1958), 130.

66. Moody, *Coming of Age*, 107.

67. Myrlie Evers-Williams and William Peters, *For Us, the Living* (Jackson, MS: Banner Books, 1996), 174.

68. John Edgar Wideman, "Looking at Emmett Till," in *In Fact: The Best of Creative Nonfiction*, ed. Lee Gutkind (New York: W. W. Norton, 2005), 25. This essay was originally published as "The Killing of Black Boys," in *Essence* (November 1997). Also see Wideman's "The Killing of Black Boys," in *The Lynching of Emmett Till*, ed. Christopher Metress (Charlottesville: University Press of Virginia, 2002), 278–88 (emphasis original).

69. Wideman, "Looking at Emmett Till," 24–48.

70. Wideman, "Looking at Emmett Till," 24.

71. Wideman, "Looking at Emmett Till," 29.

72. Wideman, "Looking at Emmett Till," 43–44.

73. Wideman, "Looking at Emmett Till," 33.

74. Wideman, "Looking at Emmett Till," 32.

75. Wideman, "Looking at Emmett Till," 33.

76. Rick Lyman, "Man Guilty of Murder in Texas Dragging Death," *New York Times*, February 24, 1998, http://www.nytimes.com/1999/02/24/us/man-guilty-of -murder-in-texas-dragging-death.html; "Man Executed for Dragging Death of James Byrd," *CNN*, September 22, 2011, http://www.cnn.com/2011/09/21/justice /texas-dragging-death-execution/; Kirk W. Fuoss, "Lynching Performances, Theatre of Violence," *Text and Performance Quarterly* 19, no. 1 (1999): 29.

77. Wideman, "Looking at Emmett Till," 31.

78. Wideman, "Looking at Emmett Till," 31.

79. Courtney Baker, "Emmett Till, Justice, and the Task of Recognition," *Journal of American Culture* 29, no. 2 (2006): 111.

Chapter Three. A Past Not Yet Passed

1. "Interviews: Andrew Roth," *Art in America Magazine*, December 22, 2009, https://www.artinamericamagazine.com/news-features/interviews/andrew-roth /. Private galleries, historical societies and cultural centers first acquired *Without Sanctuary* because more-official spaces such as national museums of art and history found its content too provocative

2. Bettina Carbonell, "The Afterlife of Lynching: Exhibitions and the Re-composition of Human Suffering," *Mississippi Quarterly* 61, no. 1/2 (2008): 197–215; Nina Burleigh, "Pictures from an Execution: An Art Gallery Tries Not to

Cause 'Sensation' with Its New Show," *New York Entertainment*, January 24, 2000, http://nymag.com/nymetro/arts/features/1828/.

3. John Pedro Schwartz, "Object Lessons: Teaching Multiliteracies through the Museum," *College English* 71, no. 1 (2008): 28; James Young, *The Texture of Memory: Holocaust Memorials and Meaning* (New Haven: Yale University Press, 1993), viii–ix.

4. Tom Hays, "Louima to Receive $8.7M," *ABC News*, July 12, 2001, http://abcnews.go.com/US/story?id=92902; "Guilty Verdict in Louima Case," *CBS News*, March 6, 2000, http://www.cbsnews.com/news/guilty-verdict-in-louima-case/; Cara Buckley, "Shades of the Louima Case in a New Claim of Abuse, with Differences," *New York Times*, October 26, 2008, http://www.nytimes.com/topic/person/abner-louima.

5. Michael Cooper, "Officers in Bronx Fire 41 Shots, and an Unarmed Man Is Killed," *New York Times*, February 5, 1999, http://www.nytimes.com/1999/02/05/nyregion/officers-in-bronx-fire-41-shots-and-an-unarmed-man-is-killed.html; Michael Grunwald, "Trial Puts Giuliani, NYPD on Defensive," *Washington Post*, March 30, 1999, http://www.washingtonpost.com/wp-srv/national/daily/march99/newyork30.htm; Jane Fritsch, "The Diallo Verdict: The Overview; 4 Officers in Diallo Shooting Are Acquitted of All Charges," *New York Times*, February 28, 2000, http://www.nytimes.com/2000/02/26/nyregion/diallo-verdict-overview-4-officers-diallo-shooting-are-acquitted-all-charges.html?pagewanted=all.

6. John Goldman, "4 White Officers Are Acquitted in Death of Diallo," *L.A. Times*, February 20, 2000, http://articles.latimes.com/2000/feb/26/news/mn-2801.

7. David Herszenhorn, "Giuliani's Response Shows a World of Difference between Two Shootings," *New York Times*, September 1, 1999, http://www.nytimes.com/1999/09/01/nyregion/giuliani-s-response-shows-a-world-of-differences-between-two-shootings.html; "No Trial for Dorismond Shooter," *CBSNews*, March 25, 2000, http://www.cbsnews.com/news/no-trial-for-dorismond-shooter/.

8. Giuliani's criticism backfired when Marie Dorismond, Patrick's mother, confirmed that Patrick was indeed an altar boy as a child. For more on Patrick Dorismond and Giuliani, see Eric Lipton, "Giuliani Cites Criminal Past of Slain Man," *New York Times*, March 20, 2000, http://www.nytimes.com/2000/03/20/nyregion/giuliani-cites-criminal-past-of-slain-man.html; Robert Hardt, "Dorismond 'Altar-Boy' Revelation Unfair: Rudy," *New York Post*, April 7, 2000, http://nypost.com/2000/04/07/dorismond-altar-boy-revelation-unfair-rudy/.

9. Maria Hinojosa, "NYC Officer Arrested in Alleged Sexual Attack on Suspect," *CNN*, April 14, 1997, http://www.cnn.com/US/9708/14/police.torture/; Buckley, "Shades of the Louima Case."

10. Stewart Desmond, "Risk and the Story of 'Without Sanctuary,'" *Museum News* (March/April 2001), 42; *Without Sanctuary*, Emory University Archives, Manuscript, Archives, and Rare Book Library, Emory University.

11. Qtd in Desmond, "Risk and the Story of 'Without Sanctuary,'" 44.

12. Discussion facilitators were trained artist-educators, historians, curators, and docents. In New York, the N-YHS hired the organization Facing History to train docents and discussion facilitators.

13. The collection's arrival in Pittsburgh came several months after a high-profile, racially motivated killing spree that left five dead and a sixth victim paralyzed. On April 28, 2000, Richard Baumhammers killed Anita Gordon, Anil Thakur, Ji-ye Sun, Theo Pham, and Garry Lee, and wounded Sandeep Patel. Anita Gordon, Baumhammers's sixty-three-year-old next-door neighbor was Jewish. After killing her, Baumhammers drove to her synagogue, spray-painted swastikas, and fired into the windows. Patel and Thakur were Indian, Sun and Pham were Asian American, and Lee was African American.

14. Jessica Gogan, "The Warhol: Museum as Artist: Creative, Dialogic and Civic Practice," http://animatingdemocracy.org/sites/default/files/andy_warhol _museum_case_study.pdf; Caroline Abels, "Lynching Photos an Exhibit Certain to Stir Emotions," *Pittsburgh Post-Gazette*, September 9, 2001; *Without Sanctuary*, Emory University Archives, Manuscript, Archives, and Rare Book Library, Emory University.

15. William Jordan, *Black Newspapers & America's War for Democracy, 1914–1920* (Chapel Hill: University of North Carolina Press, 2001), 140.

16. *Without Sanctuary: Lynching Photographs in America*, Exhibits, http://222 .museumofthenewsouth.org/exhibits/detail/?ExhibitId=118.

17. *The Clog News & Culture*, October 31, 2012, http://clclt.com/theclog/archives /2012/10/31/obama-with-noose-the-worst-halloween-decoration-ever; Brokensky, "Neighbors Angry over Obama Yard Display," November 6, 2012, http://www .city-data.com/forum/charlotte/1723234-neighbors-angry-over-obama-yard -display-8.html.

18. Tricia Couture, "Without Sanctuary: Displaying a Controversial Past," *Charlotte Viewpoint*, December 18, 2012, http://www.charlotteviewpoint.org/ article/2928/Without-Sanctuary]]-Displaying-a-controversial-pas. Like the N-YHS, curators at the Warhol sought input from members of the African American community, while local churches, the National Conference for Community Justice, and local chapters of the Urban League and the NAACP aided the museum in developing outreach programs for the public. In Detroit educational partners such as Detroit Public Schools, Michigan State University, and Wayne State University and community organizations such as the Detroit chapter of the ACLU and the National Council of Communities of Justice, as well as the Gay, Lesbian and Straight Education Network, the Urban League, and the YMCA, partnered with the Charles H. Wright Museum to develop outreach programs for the community. And in Atlanta a four-person advisory committee consisting of Emory's MARBL curator of African American Collections, Randall Burkett, and Emory University

faculty from departments of English and Law organized six discussion forums: three open to the public and three by invitation. The purpose of these open and closed discussions was to assess the public's interest in an Atlanta hosting of *Without Sanctuary* and, if receptive, to use this feedback to guide the collection's installation.

19. "Lynching Exhibit Confronts South's Ugly Past—Atlanta's Photography Collection Finally Comes Home," *Atlanta Journal-Constitution*, April 28, 2002, http://www.accessatlanta.com/ajc/metro/0402/28lynch.html.

20. "Staggers 3/7/00" Emory University Archives Series 060, *Without Sanctuary* Project Files Box 5; Folder 1: Related Events, 2000—New-York Historical Society exhibition, *Without Sanctuary* forum: February 2000, Week 4.

21. *Without Sanctuary* forum: February 2000, Week 4, February 2, 2000, Attendee Quincy. Emory University Archive Series 060, Files Box 5 Folder 1: New-York Historical Society exhibition, *Without Sanctuary* forum, *Without Sanctuary*, Emory University Archives, Manuscript, Archives, and Rare Book Library, Emory University.

22. Without Sanctuary Forum: February 2000, Week 4, February 22, 2000, Attendee Chris Easley. Emory University Archive Series 060, Files Box 5, Folder 1: New-York Historical Society exhibition *Without Sanctuary* electronic forum, *Without Sanctuary*, Emory University Archives, Manuscript, Archives, and Rare Book Library, Emory University.

23. "Without Sanctuary Forum: February 2000, Week 4," February 5, 2000, Attendee Aeysha Grice. Emory University Archive Series 060, Files Box 5, Folder 1: New-York Historical Society exhibition *Without Sanctuary* electronic forum, *Without Sanctuary*, Emory University Archives, Manuscript, Archives, and Rare Book Library, Emory University.

24. Mary Thomas, "Art Review of 'Without Sanctuary' Digs Deeply into Painful Issues of Inhumanity," *Post-Gazette*, September 29, 2001, http://old.post-gazette.com/ae/20010929thomas0929fnp5.asp.

25. Daryl White, review of *Without Sanctuary: Lynching Photography in America*, Emory University and the Martin Luther King, Jr. National Historic Site, *Public Historian* 25, no. 1 (Winter 2003): 125.

26. White, review of *Without Sanctuary*, 125.

27. Between 1901 and 1934, numerous attempts to pass federal anti-lynching legislation failed due to southern filibusters and claims that federal statute would violate states' rights. And while some states like Virginia proposed and passed an anti-lynching law (1928), most other states had no such laws, or the ones they had were circumvented by the communal dynamic present within local towns, which, more often than not, kept authorities from enforcing them. For more on coroner reports, see James Madison, *A Lynching in the Heartland* (New York: Palgrave Macmillan, 2001); Philip Dray, *At the Hands of Persons Unknown* (New York:

Random House, 2002), Cynthia Carr, *Our Town: A Heartland Lynching, a Haunted Town, and the Hidden History of White America* (New York: Crown, 2006).

28. Paul Bernish, "News Release: Freedom Center & Community Partners Announce Exhibition on the History of Lynching in America," October 19, 2009, http://freedomcenter.org/_media/pdf/WOS%20News%20Announcement% 2010-7-09%20updated.pdf.

29. Kenneth Burke, "Literature as Equipment for Living," *The Philosophy of Literary Form* (Berkeley: University of California Press, 1974), 293–304.

30. Koritha Mitchell examines lynching dramas as models of black citizenship. These plays, which were performed by all members of the black community, served as sites of social and cultural activism that modeled how to endure and survive racial violence. For more on lynching narratives as rhetorics of survival, see Koritha Mitchell, *Living with Lynching: African American Lynching Plays, Performance, and Citizenship, 1890–1930* (Champaign: University of Illinois Press, 2012); and Trudier Harris, *Exorcising Blackness: Historical and Literary Lynching and Burning Rituals* (Bloomington: Indiana University Press, 1984).

31. Kathleen Hall Jamieson and Karlyn Kohrs Campbell, "Rhetorical Hybrids: Fusions of Generic Elements," *Quarterly Journal of Speech* 68, no. 2 (1982): 147; Karen Foss, "John Lennon and the Advisory Function of Eulogies," *Central States Speech Journal* 34, no. 3 (1983): 187–94.

32. Barbie Zelizer, "Reading the Past against the Grain: The Shape of Memory Studies," *Critical Studies in Mass Communication* 12, no. 2 (1995): 214–39; Marita Sturken, *Tangled Memories: The Vietnam War Memorial, the AIDs Epidemic, and the Politics of Remembering* (Berkeley: University of California Press, 1997); Gregory Dickson, Carole Blair, and Brian Ott, *Places of Public Memory: The Rhetoric of Museums and Memorials* (Tuscaloosa: University of Alabama Press, 2010); Erica Doss, *Memorial Mania: Public Feeling in America* (Chicago: University of Chicago Press, 2010); James Young, *The Texture of Memory: Holocaust Memorials and Meaning* (New Haven: Yale University Press, 1993).

33. Charles Griswold, "The Vietnam Veterans Memorial and the Washington Mall: Philosophical Thoughts on Political Iconography," *Critical Inquiry* 12, no. 4 (1986): 689.

34. Kirk Savage, "The Past in the Present: The Life of Memorials," *Harvard Design Magazine* 9 (1999): 14.

35. Erica Doss, *Memorial Mania: Public Feeling in America* (Chicago: University of Chicago Press, 2010), 19. For more on memorials, cultural memory, and civic engagement, see Ekaterina Haskins, *Popular Memories: Commemoration, Participatory Culture, and Democratic Citizenship* (Columbia: University of South Carolina Press, 2015).

36. Wendy Wolters, "Without Sanctuary: Bearing Witness, Bearing Whiteness," *JAC* 24, no. 2 (2004): 402.

37. Wolters, "Without Sanctuary," 410.

38. Wolters, "Without Sanctuary," 410.

39. Elizabeth Grace Hale, review of *Without Sanctuary: Lynching Photography in America, Journal of American History* 89, no. 3 (December 2002), 989–94.

40. Qtd. in Robert E. Snyder, "Without Sanctuary: An American Holocaust?," *Southern Quarterly: A Journal of the Arts in the South* 39, no. 3 (2001): 167–68.

41. Hale, review, 993; Wolters, "Without Sanctuary"; qtd. in Snyder, "Without Sanctuary: An American Holocaust?" 162–71.

42. Qtd. in Barbie Zelizer, *Remembering to Forget: Holocaust Memory through the Camera's Eye* (Chicago: University of Chicago Press, 1998), 10.

43. "Senate Apologizes for Inaction on Lynchings: Lawmakers Express Contrition for Condoning 'This Terrorism in America,'" *NBC News*, June 13, 2005, http://www.nbcnews.com/id/8206697/ns/us_news-life/t/senate-apologizes -inaction-lynchings/#.WXe7Qao-LOY.

44. Qtd. in "History, Horror, Healing: Faculty Deliberations on Lynching Photography Examine Racial and Historical Understanding," *Academic Exchange*, http://www.emory.edu/ACAD_EXCHANGE/2001/aprmay/horror.html.

45. Zelizer, Remembering to Forget, 10.

46. Joshua Lazerson, "Lynching Exhibit Comments," *LA Times*, August 30, 2000, http://articles.latimes.com/2000/aug/30/local/me-12446.

Chapter Four. Lynching in the Age of Obama

1. Ta-Nehisi Coates, "Fear of a Black President," *Atlantic*, September 8, 2012, http://www.theatlantic.com/magazine/archive/2012/09/fear-of-a-black-president/309064/.

2. Toni Morrison, "Comment," *New Yorker*, October 5, 1998, http://www .newyorker.com/magazine/1998/10/05/comment-6543.

3. Barack Obama, "2004 DNC Keynote Address," July 27, 2007, http://www .washingtonpost.com/wp-dyn/articles/A19751-2004Jul27.html.

4. Patricia Williams, *Alchemy of Race & Rights* (Cambridge: Harvard University Press, 1991); Charles Mills, *The Racial Contract* (Ithaca: Cornel University Press, 1997); Joel Olson, *Abolition of White Democracy* (Minneapolis: University of Minnesota Press, 2004).

5. Joseph Lowndes, "Barack Obama's Body: The Presidency, the Body Politic, and the Contest over American National Identity," *Polity* 45, no. 4 (2013): 470.

6. Tom Namako, "I Was a Clinton Volunteer," *Huffington Post*, April 26, 2008, http:// www.huffingtonpost.com/tom-namako/i-was-a-clinton-volunteer_b_97526.html.

7. Nathan Thornburgh, "Why Is Obama's Middle Name Taboo?" *Content*, February 28, 2008, http://content.time.com/time/politics/article/0,8599,1718255,00 .html; Geekesque, "HillaryClinton.com Spreading Obama=Muslim Smears and Other Racism," *DailyKos*, March 14, 2008, https://www.dailykos.com/story/2008 /3/14/476539/-.

8. Qtd. in Cornell Belcher, *A Black Man in the White House: Barack Obama and the Triggering of America's Racial-Aversion Crisis* (Healdsburg, CA: Water Street Press, 2016), 79; Jennifer Senior, "Dreaming of Obama," *Nymag.com*, October 2, 2007, http://nymag.com/nymag/features/21681/index7.html.

9. Amy Holyfield, "Obama's Birth Certificate: Final Chapter," *Politifact.com*, June 27, 2008, http://www.politifact.com/truth-o-meter/article/2008/jun/27/obamas -birth-certificate-part-ii/.

10. Sammy Alim Geneva Smitherman, *Articulate while Black: Barack Obama, Language, and Race in the U.S.* (Oxford: Oxford University Press, 2012), 94, 96.

11. Larry McShane, "Barack and Michelle Obama's 'Fist Bump of Hope' Shows Them Silly in Love," *New York Daily News*, June 6, 2008, http://www.nydailynews. com/news/politics/barack-michelle-obama-fist-bump-hope-shows-silly-love-arti-cle-1.295037; Rachel Sklar, "Obama Fist-Bump Rocks the Nation!" *Huffington Post*, June 14, 2008, http://www.huffingtonpost.com/2008/06/06/obama-fist-bump-rocks -the_n_105490.html.

12. Susanne Goldenberg, "U.S. Election: 'Terrorist Fist Bump' Cartoon Backfires," *Guardian*, July 14, 2008, https://www.theguardian.com/world/2008/jul/15 /barackobama.usa; Rachel Sklar, "Yikes! Controversial *New Yorker* Cover Shows Muslim, Flag-Burning, Osama-Loving, Fist-Bumping Obama," July 18, 2008, http:// www.huffingtonpost.com/2008/07/13/yikes-controversial-emnew_n_112429.html; "Fox Anchor Calls Obama Fist Pound a "Terrorist Fist Jab," *Huffington Post*, June 17, 2008, http://www.huffingtonpost.com/2008/06/09/fox-anchor-calls-obama-fi_ n_106027.html; Jim Ruttenberg, "Deconstructing the Bump," *New York Times*, June 11, 2008, https://thecaucus.blogs.nytimes.com/2008/06/11/deconstructing-the -bump/?mcubz=1&mcubz=1&_r=0.

13. Sklar, "Yikes! Controversial *New Yorker*," http://www.huffingtonpost. com/2008/07/13/yikes-controversial-emnew_n_112429.html; David Remnick, "On That *New Yorker* Cover: It's Satire, Meant to Target 'Distortions and Misconceptions and Prejudices' about Obama," *Huffington Post*, July 21, 2008, http://www.huffington post.com/2008/07/13/david-remnick-on-emnew-yo_n_112456.html.

14. Nico Pitney, "Barry Britt Defends His *New Yorker* Cover Art of Obama," July 21, 2008, http://www.huffingtonpost.com/2008/07/13/barry-blitt-addresses-his_n_ 112432.html.

15. Brent Staples, "Just Walk On By," http://www.myteacherpages.com/webpages /rspriggs/files/staples%20just%20walk%20on%20by%20text.pdf.

16. Keith Erickson, "Presidential Rhetoric's Visual Turn: Performance Fragments and the Politics of Illusionism," in *Visual Rhetoric: A Reader in Communication and American Culture*, ed. Lester Olson, Carra Finnegan, and Diane Hope (Los Angeles: SAGE, 2008), 360.

17. Erickson, "Presidential Rhetoric's Visual Turn," 360 (emphasis original).

18. Erickson, "Presidential Rhetoric's Visual Turn," 360.

19. Janny Scott, "Obama Chooses Reconciliation over Rancor," *New York Times*, March 19, 2008, http://www.nytimes.com/2008/03/19/us/politics/19assess.html.

20. Susan Sarapin, "Obama's Pastor Disaster and Apologia by Proxy: A Change in Structure for Image Restoration," paper presented at the annual meeting of the NCA 95th Annual Convention, Chicago Hilton and Towers, Chicago, November 11, 2009.

21. Barack Obama, "A More Perfect Union," speech delivered March 18, 2008, Philadelphia, PA, *AmericanRhetoric*, http://www.americanrhetoric.com/speeches/barackobamaperfectunion.htm; "Transcript of Obama Speech," *Politico*, http://www.politico.com/story/2008/03/transcript-of-obama-speech-009100.

22. Obama, "More Perfect Union."

23. Williams, *Alchemy*, 1992; Michael Omi and Howard Winant, *Racial Formation in the United States: From the 1960s to the 1990s* (New York: Routledge, 1989; Mills, *Racial Contract*; Roxanne Mountford, *The Gendered Pulpit: Preaching in American Protestant Spaces* (Carbondale: University of Southern Illinois Press, 2005); Eduardo Bonilla-Silva et al., "When Whites Flock Together: The Social Psychology of White Habitus," *Critical Sociology* 32, no. 2–3 (2006): 229–53.

24. Dick Durbin, "Senator Durbin Introduces Obama," *YouTube*. https://www.youtube.com/watch?v=rgZCz-GbPWo.

25. Durbin, "Senator Durbin Introduces Obama."

26. Daniel Berkowitz and Sarah Raaii, "Conjuring Abraham, Martin and John: Memory and News of the Obama Presidential Campaign, *Memory Studies* 3, no. 4 (2010): 366.

27. Durbin, "Senator Durbin Introduces Obama."

28. "About Our Christian University," http://www.georgefox.edu/about/mission_vision_values/index.html.

29. Wood, *Lynching and Spectacle*, 48. Also see Peter Ehrenhaus and Susan A. Owen, "Race Lynching and Christian Evangelicalism: Performances of Faith," *Text & Performance Quarterly* 24, no. 3 (2004): 276–301.

30. "Obama Effigy Found Hanging from Campus Tree," *Associated Press* September 24, 2008, http://www.msnbc.msn.com/id/26872774/ns/us_news-life; Julia Hoppock, "Ore. School Says Students Confess to Hanging Obama Effigy from Tree," *ABC News*, October 1, 2008, http://www.msnbc.msn.com/id/26872774/ns/us_news-life.

31. "Racist Obama Effigy Hung in Ohio" (video), *Huffington Post*, November 19, 2008, https://www.huffingtonpost.com/2008/10/19/racist-obama-effigy-hung_n_135971.html; "Scary Obama Ghost Hangs from Tree Racist," http://www.youtube.com/watch?v=XSFfEcj3uFY&feature=youtube_gdata_player; "Ohio Neighbors Upset over Anti-Obama Ghost," http://current.com/entertainment/wtf/89419260_ohio-neighbors-upset-over-anti-obama-ghost.htm.

32. "Lawyer: Men 'Extremely Sorry' for Ky. Effigy Prank," *San Diego Union Tribune*, October 31, 2008, http://www.sandiegouniontribune.com/sdut-obama-effigy-10-31-08-2008oct31-story.html.

33. "2 Men Voice Remorse for Hanging Obama Effigy," *Deseret News*, November 1, 2008, http://www.deseretnews.com/article/705259622/2-men-voice-remorse-for-hanging-Obama-effigy.html.

34. *INC Now 24/7 News Source*, October 30, 2008, http://www.indianasnewscenter.com/news/local/33566224.html; Peter Ambrose, "Man Hangs Effigy of Barack Obama on Tree," October 30, 2008, http://www.wpta21.com/story/33533253/man-hangs-effigy-of-barack-obama-on-tree.

Conclusion: A Civic Tradition Continued

1. Yancy, *Look, a White!, Philosophical Essays on Whiteness* (Philadelphia: Temple University Press, 2012), 21.

2. Jason Howerton, "Anti-Obama Signs Ignite Controversy: 'Somewhere in Kenya, a Village Is Missing Its Idiot,'" *TheBlaze* August 30, 2012, http://www.theblaze.com/news/2012/08/30/anti-obama-signs-ignite-controversy-somewhere-in-kenya-a-village-is-missing-its-idiot/; Steve Frank, "Anti-Obama Billboard: 'Somewhere in Kenya, a Village Is Missing Its Idiot,'" *MSNBC*, August 30, 2012, http://www.msnbc.com/the-ed-show/anti-obama-billboard-somewhere-keny.

3. Michael Hainey, "Clint and Scott Eastwood: No Holds Barred in Their First Interview Together," *Esquire*, August 3, 2016, http://www.esquire.com/entertainment/a46893/double-trouble-clint-and-scott-eastwood/; Meryl Gottlieb, "Clint Eastwood Finally Explains His Infamous Empty-Chair Speech and Calls It 'Silly,'" *Business Insider*, August 3, 2016, http://www.businessinsider.com/clint-eastwood-explains-empty-chair-speech-at-2012-rnc-2016-8.

4. "Hey Everyone, It's 'Empty Chair Lynching'!" *The Godless Liberal*, September 22, 2012, http://thegodlessliberal.blogspot.com/2012/09/hey-everyone-its-empty-chair-lynching.html; Roz Plater, "Centerville Man Says Lynching Not Implied by Hanging 'Nobama' Chair from Tree," *WJLA*, Washington, DC, September 20, 2012, http://wjla.com/news/local/centreville-man-says-lynching-not-implied-by-hanging-nobama-chair-from-tree-80121.

5. Nick Wing, "Laura Mulholland, Minnesota Woman, Impales Chair with Bayonet, 'Lynches' It in Anti-Obama Display," *Huffington Post*, October 31, 2012, http://www.huffingtonpost.com/2012/10/31/laura-mulholland-chair-lynching-bayonet_n_2050766.html.

6. Eduardo Bonilla-Silva, *Racism without Racists* (Lanham, MD: Rowman and Littlefield, 2009); Joel Olson, *Abolition of White Democracy* (Minneapolis: University of Minnesota Press, 2004).

7. David Sherfinski, "Va. Man: No Lynching Connotations to Strung-Up 'Nobama' Chair," *Washington Times*, September 21, 2012, http://www.washington times.com/blog/inside-politics/2012/sep/21/va-man-no-lynching-connotations-strung-nobama-chai/; Stevie Mathieu, "Chair Hangs from Tree in Camas Anti-Obama Protest, Local GOP Denounces Display Similar to 'Chair Lynchings' Seen in Other States," *Columbian*, October 3, 2012, http://www.columbian.com/news/2012/oct/03/chair-lynching-obama-racism/.

8. Eric Ortiz, "Is This an Anti-Obama Lynching? Texas Man Hangs Chair from Tree Inspired by Clint Eastwood Speech," *New York Daily News*, September 21, 2012, http://www.nydailynews.com/news/politics/anti-obama-lynching-texas-man-hangs-chair-tree-inspired-clint-eastwood-speech-article-1.1164520; Sherfinski, "Va. Man"; Madeleine Morgenstern, " 'It's Not a Lynch!' Fiery TX Man Takes Down Hanging Empty Chair Representing Obama in Front of News Crew," *TheBlaze*, September 21, 2012, http://www.theblaze.com/news/2012/09/21/its-not-a-lynch-fiery-tx-man-takes-down-hanging-empty-chair-representing-obama-in-front-of-news-crew/.

9. Bonilla-Silva, *Racism without Racists*, 77.

10. Mathieu, "Chair Hangs from Tree."

11. Bonilla-Silva, *Racism without Racists*.

12. Barack Obama, "Remarks from the President on Trayvon Martin," July 19, 2013, https://www.whitehouse.gov/the-press-office/2013/07/19/remarks-president-trayvon-martin.

13. "Transcript: Obama's Remarks on Race, Trayvon Martin," *CBS News*, July 19, 2013, http://www.cbsnews.com/news/transcript-obamas-remarks-on-race-trayvon-martin/2/.

14. "MSNBC Guest: Zimmerman's Defense Was Protecting 'White Womanhood' from Trayvon," *RealClearPolitics.com*, July 14, 2013, http://www.realclearpolitics.com/video/2013/07/14/msnbc_guest_zimmermans_defense_was_protecting_white_womanhood_from_trayvon.html; Nathan Roush, "Blogger Mychal Denzel Smith Equates Zimmerman Defense with Justifying Lynching," *MCR News Busters*, July 19, 2013, http://www.newsbusters.org/blogs/nathan-roush/2013/07/19/blogger-mychal-denzel-smith-equates-zimmerman-defense-justifying-lynch.

15. Melanie Morrison, "Trayvon Martin, the Legacy of Lynching, and the Role of White Women," *Melanie M Morrison* (2014), http://alliesforchange.org/documents/trayvon-martin-legacy-of-lynching-and-role-of-white-women.pdf.

16. Isabel Wilkerson, "Mike Brown's Shooting and Jim Crow Lynchings Have Too Much in Common: It's Time for America to Own Up," August 25, 2014, http://www.theguardian.com/commentisfree/2014/aug/25/mike-brown-shooting-jim-crow-lynchings-in-common.

17. Karen Johnson and Kenneth Johnson, "Looking-Like Trayvon," *(Re)Teaching Trayvon: Education for Racial Justice and Human Freedom*, ed. Venus E. Evans-Winters and Magaela C. Bethune (Rotterdam: Sense, 2014), 25.

18. Taryn Galbreath, "Angela Bassett Speaks at St. Sabrina," *Chicago Defender*, April 4, 2012, https://chicagodefender.com/2012/04/04/angela-bassett-speaks-hellip-2105/.

19. Roslyn Brock, "NAACP Department of Justice Petition," *NAACP.org*, July 8, 2013, http://www.naacp-riverside.org/articles/naacp-department-justice-petition.

20. Anthony Brown and Marcus Johnson, "Blackness Enclosed: Understanding the Trayvon Martin Incident through the Long History of Black Male Imagery," in *(Re)Teaching Trayvon: Education for Racial Justice and Human Freedom*, ed. Venus E. Evans-Winters and Magaela C. Bethune (Rotterdam: Sense, 2014), 11.

21. Amanda Sloane and Graham Winch, "Key Witness Recounts Trayvon Martin's Final Phone Call," *CNN*, June 27, 2013, http://www.cnn.com/2013/06/26/justice/zimmerman-trial/.

22. Qtd. in George Yancy and Janine Jones, *Pursuing Trayvon: Historical Contexts and Contemporary Manifestations of Racial Dynamics* (Lanham, MD: Lexington Books, 2014), 2–3; Adam Weinstein and MoJo News Team, "The Trayvon Martin Killing, Explained," *Mother Jones*, March 18, 2012, https://www.motherjones.com/politics/2012/03/what-happened-trayvon-martin-explained/

23. Jack Mirkinson, "Oprah: Trayvon Martin the 'Same Thing' as Emmett Till" (video), *Huffpost Black Voices*, May 5, 2013, http://www.huffingtonpost.com/2013/08/05/oprah-trayvon-martin-emmett-till_n_3707096.html. For more on this analogy, see Yancy and Jones, *Pursuing Trayvon Martin* (2013); Nicolaus Mills, "A Longer Look at the Emmett Till–Trayvon Martin Comparison," *Huffpost Black Voices*, July 17, 2013, http://www.huffingtonpost.com/nicolaus-mills/emmett-till-trayvon-martin_b_3606636.html; Jason Howerton, "Oprah's Stunning Trayvon Martin Comparison: 'In My Mind, Same Thing,'" *TheBlaze*, August 5, 2013, https://www.theblaze.com/news/2013/08/05/oprahs-stunning-trayvon-martin-comparison-in-my-mind-same-thing; Kevin Alexander Gray, Jeffrey St. Clair, and JoAnn Wypijewski, eds., *Killing Trayvons: An Anthology of American Violence* (Petrolia, CA: Counterpunch, 2014); *Cultural Studies–Critical Methodologies* Special Issue: "From Emmett Till to Trayvon Martin," 15, no. 4 (2015): 239–321.

24. Kenneth Burke, *Counterstatement* (Berkeley: University of California Press, 1968), 143–60.

25. Lottie Joiner, "How Emmett Till Changed the World," *Daily Beast*, August 28, 2015, http://www.thedailybeast.com/how-emmett-till-changed-the-world; Charles

Blow, "60 Years Later, Echoes of Emmett Till's Killing," *New York Times*, August 31, 2015, http://nyti.ms/1JvL9Uw.

26. Truider Harris, *Exorcising Blackness: Historical and Literary Lynching and Burning Rituals* (Bloomington: Indiana University Press, 1984).

27. Amy Green, "Zimmerman's Twin Lakes Community Was on Edge before Trayvon Shooting," *Daily Beast*, March 28, 2012, https://www.thedailybeast.com /zimmermans-twin-lakes-community-was-on-edge-before-trayvon-shooting; Ian Tuttle, "The Neighborhood Zimmerman Watched," *National Review*, July 22, 2013, http://www.nationalreview.com/article/354042/neighborhood-zimmerman -watched-ian-tuttle.

28. Cynthia Skove Nevels, *Lynching to Belong: Claiming Whiteness through Racial Violence* (College Station: Texas A&M University Press, 2007).

29. Lewis Gordon, "The Irreplaceability of Continued Struggle," in George Yancy and Janine Jones, *Pursuing Trayvon: Historical Contexts and Contemporary Manifestations of Racial Dynamics* (Lanham, MD: Lexington Books, 2014), 86.

30. Frank Wilderson, "The Prison Slave as Hegemony's (Silent) Scandal," *Social Justice* 30, no. 2 (2003): 18.

31. Edward J. Blakely and Mary Gail Snyder, *Fortress America: Gated Communities in the United States* (Washington, DC: Brookings Institution Press, 1997); Matthew Durington, "Race, Space and Place in Suburban Durban: An Ethnographic Assessment of Gated Community Environments and Residents," *GeoJournal* 66, no. 1/2 (2006): 147–60; Joe Morgan, "Gated Communities: Institutionalizing Social Stratification," *Geographical Bulletin* 54 (2013): 24–36; Elena Vesselinov, Matthew Cazessus, and William Falk, "Gated Communities and Spatial Inequality," *Journal of Urban Affairs* 2 (2007): 109–27.

32. George Yancy, *Look, a White!*, 17–50.

33. Safia Ali, "Fired Officer Who Shot Tamir Rice Could Be Back at Another Department," *NBC News*, June 2, 2017, https://www.nbcnews.com/news/us-news /fired-officer-who-shot-tamir-rice-could-be-back-another-n766921.

34. The wrongful death settlements of black men from 1999 to 2016 ranged between 1.5 million and 6 million dollars. For more on wrongful death settlements of unarmed black men, see Ryllie Danylko, "Tamir Rice Settlement: How Cleveland's $6 Million Payout Compares with Similar Cases in US," *Cleveland.com*, April 25, 2016, http://www.cleveland.com/metro/index.ssf/2016/04/how_the_tamir _rice_settlement.html; Jim Salter, "Ferguson Attorney: Brown Family Wrongful Death Settlement Is $1.5 Million," *Chicago Tribune*, June 24, 2017, http://www .chicagotribune.com/news/nationworld/ct-ferguson-brown-family-settlement -20170623-story.html; Amy Forliti, "Philando Castile Family Reaches $3M Settlement in Death, *Chicago Tribune*, June 26, 2017, http://www.chicagotribune .com/news/nationworld/ct-philando-castile-death-settlement-20170626-story.html; William Glaberson, "City Settles Suit in Guard's Death by Police Bullet," *New York*

Times, March 13, 2003, http://www.nytimes.com/2003/03/13/nyregion/city-settles
-suit-in-guard-s-death-by-police-bullet.html.

35. Dave Zirin, "Why I Called the Murder of Richard Collins III a 'Lynching,'"
Nation, May 25, 2017, https://www.thenation.com/article/called-murder-richard
-collins-iii-lynching/.

36. Frank Shay, *Judge Lynch: The First Hundred Years* (New York: Ives Washburn,
1938), 99.

Postscript: Caught Up

1. Ray Stern, "The Battle Isn't Over between ASU Professor and Cop Who
Arrested Her in 2014," *Phoenix New Times*, January 28, 2018, http://www.phoenix
newtimes.com/news/asu-professor-ersula-ore-says-cop-who-arrested-her-in-2014
-on-deadly-path-10068594.

2. Stern, "The Battle Isn't Over"; Ray Stern, "Bad Math: Pinal Data Worse than
Reported on Deputy Who Abused ASU Professor," *Phoenix New Times*, February 1,
2018, http://www.phoenixnewtimes.com/news/pinal-county-deputy-targeted-by
-asu-professor-has-higher-complaint-average-10093973.

3. Stern, "Bad Math."

4. Jerome Karabel, "Police Killings Surpass the Worst Years of Lynching, Capital
Punishment, and a Movement Responds," *Huffington Post*, December 6, 2017,
https://www.huffingtonpost.com/jerome-karabel/police-killings-lynchings-capital
-punishment_b_8462778.html.

5. "The Cop Who Killed Antwon Rose Violated the Civil Rights of Others, a
New Lawsuit Claims," *Mother Jones*, July 3, 2018.

INDEX

CPSIA information can be obtained
at www.ICGtesting.com
Printed in the USA
BVHW072126221220
596252BV00004B/20